Colonial America

VOLUME 9

Rhode Island—Stamp Act Crisis

CONSULTANT EDITOR: DR. D. THORP

Published 1998 by
Grolier Educational, Sherman Turnpike, Danbury, Connecticut 06816

Reprinted in 2001

© 1998 Brown Partworks Ltd

Set ISBN: 0-7172-9193-6
Volume ISBN: 0-7172-9202-9

Library of Congress Cataloging-in-Publication Data
Colonial America.
p.cm.—Includes bibliographical references and index.
Contents: v. 1. A-By—v. 2.C-De—v. 3. Di-Ga—v. 4. Ge-In—
v. 5. In-Marq—v. 6. Marr-Na—v. 7. Ne-Pe—v. 8. Ph-Re—
v. 9. Rh-St—v. 10. St-Z.

1. United States—History—Colonial period, ca. 1600–1775—
Encyclopedias. Juvenile. 2. United States—History—Revolution,
1775–1783—Encyclopedias. Juvenile. I. Grolier Educational (Firm)
II. Title: Colonial America.
E188.C696   1998
973.2—DC21   97-44595
                                                                       CIP
                                                                        AC

For information address the publisher:
Grolier Educational, Sherman Turnpike, Danbury, Connecticut 06816

FOR BROWN PARTWORKS LTD
Editor: Clint Twist
Designer: Bradley Davis
Picture research: Sharon Southren
Text editor: Mike Sharpe

Printed in Singapore

CONTENTS

RHODE ISLAND

Rhode Island, the smallest British colony in America, was one of the New World's most diverse communities. Founded by men and women in search of basic freedoms, Rhode Island developed into a colonial haven for independent thought. Its dedication to the principle of free thinking made the tiny New England settlement a trend-setter for colonial America.

Before European colonization of Rhode Island began, several Native-American tribes inhabited the area. These tribes included the Niantic, Nipmuck, Pequot, Wampanoag, and Narragansett. All were members of the Algonquian language family, North America's largest group of Native-American tribes. The Narragansett tribe left a particularly strong legacy, as their name graces the beautiful Narragansett Bay, the large inlet that nearly bisects Rhode Island.

Before the founding of a permanent European settlement several explorers visited the Rhode Island region. In 1502 the Portugese explorer Miguel Corte Real may have sailed along the coast to become the first European to see the area. Italian Giovanni da Verrazano visited the region in 1524. Dutch explorer Adriaen Block landed in the area in 1614 and traded for furs, but neither he nor any of those before him established a colony in the region.

ROGER WILLIAMS

The first individual to found a settlement in the Rhode Island area was Roger Williams. In 1635 Massachusetts leaders expelled Williams from their colony because of religious differences. This forced Williams to flee Massachusetts. In 1636 he bought a parcel of land from the Narragansett tribe and founded the town of Providence. In this settlement Williams intended to create a place of religious freedom.

In 1644, and again in 1663, Roger Williams acquired a charter for the colony of Rhode Island. Both charters served two important purposes. First, they legally established the idea of religious freedom within Rhode Island's borders. Second, the charter protected Rhode Island from neighboring colonies. Massachusetts posed the most serious threat to Rhode Island because Puritan leaders wished to put an end to the tiny settlement. By obtaining the two

▲ *Roger Williams purchased the land he required to build the city of Providence from the Narragansett.*

R

charters, Williams secured Rhode Island's independent future.

EARLY SETTLEMENT

Rhode Island's promise of religious freedom soon attracted many persecuted individuals. In 1638 a group of religious outcasts followed Anne Hutchinson from Massachusetts into Rhode Island. This group founded the town of Portsmouth. A few years later another small band of outcasts founded Newport.

The legal right to freedom of religion lured many other groups to Williams's colony. In 1639 a group of Baptists settled in Providence and organized the first Baptist church in America. Large groups of Quakers and Jews also moved to the colony. Although these groups suffered intense persecution in other colonies, they enjoyed freedom and toleration in Rhode Island.

In the 1670s Native Americans posed a serious challenge to Rhode Island's existence. For decades European settlers and native tribes had lived peacefully in Rhode Island.

As the European population grew, however, Native Americans felt increasingly threatened. Their fears led to the conflict known as King Philip's War between 1675 and 1678. The settlers won an early battle known as the Great Swamp Fight, but the natives quickly retaliated with victories of their own. Metacom, the Native-American leader, was killed, and the colonists secured a peace and retained the territory of Rhode Island.

▲ *The town meetinghouse (known as "The Abbott House") in Providence that was used by Roger Williams.*

◄ *Old Harbor on Block Island, which lies about 10 miles (16 km) off the coast of Rhode Island. Block Island was named after the Dutch explorer Adriaen Block and is also known by its Native-American name Manisses (or Manassses). The island was settled by emigrants from Massachusetts in 1661.*

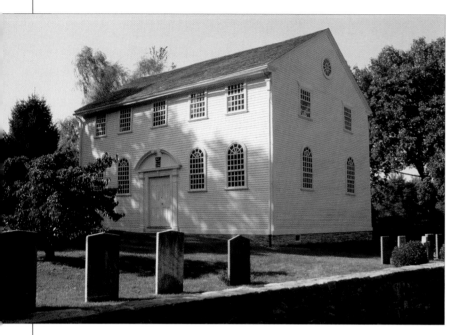

Newport became an especially active slave-trading location. For many years Rhode Island generated tremendous profits from the slave trade.

In 1774, however, Rhode Island chose to ignore the lure of profits and became the first colony in America to prohibit the importation of slaves. When the slave trade ended, the colony's economy changed. Many ship owners turned from the slaving to whaling. This decision helped make Providence and Newport leading American whaling centers. Many merchants turned to industry. In 1787 America's first cotton-spinning machine was built in Providence. In a few short years Rhode Island became an American industrial leader.

RHODE ISLAND REBELLION
While the colony attempted to concentrate on economic growth, problems with Britain began to arise. During the 1760s British officials

In the years following the defeat of Metacom Rhode Island's economy flourished. Large southern-style plantations arose on the colony's fertile coastal lands. These plantations specialized in raising livestock, especially cattle and sheep. In addition, plantation owners developed a fine breed of horse, the famous Narragansett Pacer.

The colony's most important source of income was shipping. Many impressive ports lined Rhode Island's coast, and the colonists used these ports to their full advantage. Throughout the 18th century Rhode Island merchants carried exports to the West Indies, where they commanded favorable prices.

SLAVERY AND WHALING
As Rhode Island's economy blossomed, the colonists added a new element to the mix—slavery. Throughout the 1700s Rhode Island farms contained a sizable slave population. Rhode Island merchants used slavery to their advantage as well. By investing in the African slave trade, these merchants linked their own ships and ports to the trade.

▲ *The Old Narragansett Church was built in 1707 in Wickford, Rhode Island.*

▶ *The Colony House was built in Newport, Rhode Island, in 1739 as the seat of the colonial government. After the Revolutionary War it served as the state capitol, in alternate years, until 1900.*

imposed severe taxes on the American colonies. In addition Britain placed limits on colonial trade, a policy that angered Rhode Islanders.

The citizens of Rhode Island became the first colonists to retaliate against British policies and to take action against British rule. In 1769 Rhode Islanders burned the British ship *Liberty* while it was anchored at Newport. On June 22, 1772, men from Providence destroyed the British warship *Gaspee*, an act that excited and aroused public opinion throughout colonial America. On May 4, 1776, Rhode Island became the first colony to declare its independence.

As the Revolutionary War raged, several Rhode Islanders made important contributions. Stephen Hopkins was the chief organizer of the Continental Navy, and Esek Hopkins became the Navy's first commander-in-chief. One of the Continental Army's most famous generals, Nathanael Greene, also called Rhode Island home.

Once America achieved independence, Rhode Island tended to act separately from the other states in the Union. Most Rhode Islanders wished to maintain control over their own state's affairs. They feared that a strong federal government could take away the rights of the state and the rights of individuals. These fears led Rhode Island to reject the United States Constitution on March 24, 1788. Rhode Island continued to reject the Constitution until the Bill of Rights was added. Finally on May 29, 1790, Rhode Island became the last of the 13 original states to ratify, or approve, the United States Constitution.

SEE ALSO

ALGONQUIAN ■ AMERICAN REVOLUTIONARY WAR ■ HUTCHINSON, ANNE ■ KING PHILIP'S WAR ■ LIVESTOCK ■ MASSACHUSETTS ■ SLAVE TRADE ■ WILLIAMS, ROGER

▶ *Rebellious colonists watch the British warship* Gaspee *burn off Rhode Island in 1772.*

R RICE

◄ *Native-American women gather wild rice from a birch-bark canoe. The woman in the center is using a wooden club to crudely thresh the rice grains from the stalks.*

Wild rice is the only cereal native to what is now the United States. Wild rice is a grass, only distantly related to cultivated rice. It grows naturally in the lake beds of the upper Midwest and is harvested today by the Ojibway tribes in much the same way it was in the 1600s.

The first Native Americans known to harvest wild rice were Siouan and Algonquian peoples. The French priest Father Claude Jean Allouez wrote in his journal in 1666 that the Native Americans he encountered "were much more nomadic than any of the other nations, having no fixed abode, no fields, no villages, and living wholly on game and a small quantity of oats (wild rice) which they gather in marshy places."

The French referred to the wild rice as "folle avoine" or "wild oats." Europeans exploring in North America often compared it to oats or rye. When the Ojibway moved into the Lake Superior region of northern Minnesota and southern Canada to take advantage of the fur trade with the French, they began harvesting the wild rice to provide a supplement to their diet of fish and game.

RICE PLANTATIONS

Cultivated rice was introduced into North America in 1685. The seed for the rice had come from Madagascar, an island in the Indian Ocean. Sugar plantation owners from Barbados, who moved to South Carolina looking for more land and opportunity, were the first to experiment with large-scale rice production.

The rice plantations became dependent on slave labor because growing rice is very labor intensive. Much of the work is concerned with the maintainance of the numerous irrigation channels that rice cultivation requires. Many of the slaves who were brought to South Carolina were from the west coast of Africa, where rice is grown. The slaves brought to rice

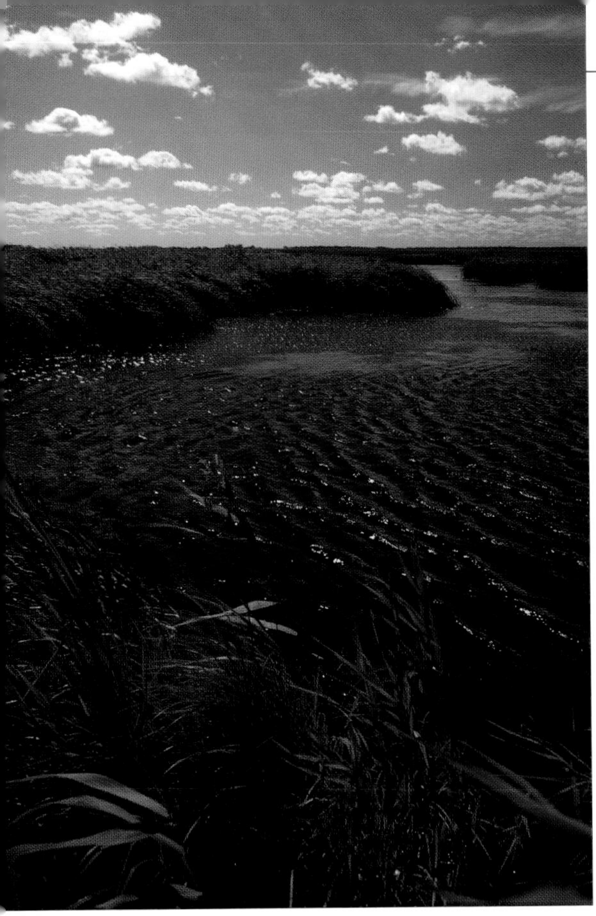

Wild rice growing in the shallows along the margins of Turtle Lake, Minnesota.

plantations probably had a significant impact on the development of the rice industry in North America because they knew more about rice cultivation than their white owners.

Rice was grown in the tidal swamps, where fresh water was influenced by the rising and falling tide. The perfection of the system of flooding and draining the rice fields was the breakthrough that made rice cultivation possible on land that was otherwise useless for agriculture.

RICE EXPORTS

Rice was an enumerated export until 1730. The British insisted that all rice exported from the colonies had to be shipped to Britain. The cargo was then reexported to Spain, Portugal, Italy, Holland, and Germany where it was eaten as a low-cost substitute for bread. From 1730, after many appeals, the British allowed rice to be exported directly to southern Europe.

Rice became one of the main export commodities from the colonies in the late 18th century. Eighty percent of all the rice was shipped out of Charleston, helping it to grow into the fourth largest city in the British colonies by 1776.

Rice growing moved into Georgia in 1750 after the prohibition on slavery in that colony ended. Although rice grew well in Georgia, South Carolina remained the biggest colonial producer of rice.

SEE ALSO
FARMING ■ GEORGIA ■ INDIGO ■ LAND ■ PLANTATIONS ■ SLAVE CULTURE ■ SLAVERY ■ SOUTH CAROLINA

A 19th-century illustration of black fieldworkers threshing rice on a North Carolina plantation.

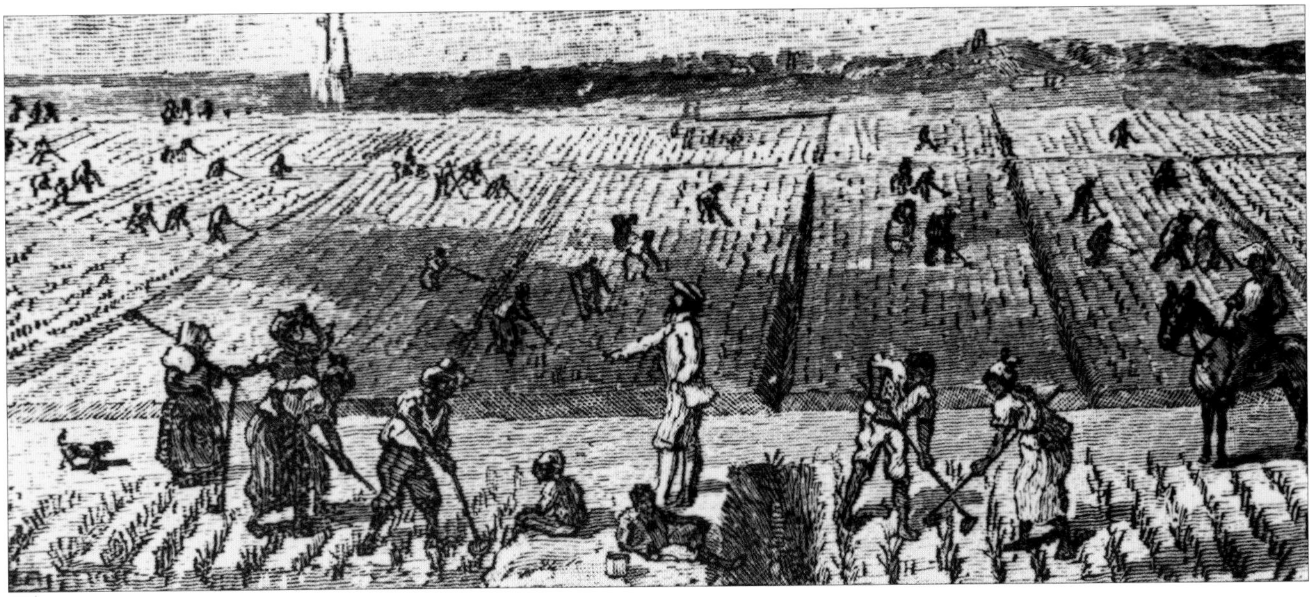

R RIVER TRAVEL

Rivers and the coastal waters of bays and sounds provided the fastest, easiest, and most efficient transportation for all Americans throughout the colonial period. As late as 1775 the average European settlement was no further than 70 miles (113 km) inland, and a string of cities—Boston, New York, Philadelphia, and Charleston—all developed and prospered because of harbor locations. Another string of cities had arisen farther west: Trenton, New Jersey; Hartford, Connecticut; Richmond, Virginia; and Augusta, Georgia. These cities were all located along fall lines, the points on inland waterways that marked the upstream limit for ocean-going vessels.

NATIVE CANOES
Long before the arrival of European settlers Native Americans had used the waterways for transportation and to develop trading networks over great distances. Their vehicle was the canoe, made either from a hollowed-out log or the bark of the birch tree. Rock paintings (petroglyphs) hundreds of years old have been discovered that show natives using canoes. In 1712 a European traveler marveled at the natives' remarkable ability to make a canoe "in less than half a day...of the bark of trees."

French fur traders quickly adopted the use of birch bark canoes. Using them as a means of transportation, the French pushed far to the west with their trade routes. Settlers in the Louisiana bayous also adapted the Native-American vehicle of transportation when they hollowed out cypress logs to make pirogues.

EUROPEAN BOATS
In other areas of North America European-style vessels were changed to fit new conditions. The Chesapeake Bay region, with its hundreds of bays, creeks, and rivers, gave rise to Bermuda sloops and small coastal "shallops"—a type of small, open boat with both a sail and oars. In Virginia sea-faring vessels were so important that specific laws detailed what should be done if a person found a boat, and how a person should go about claiming a "stray" boat.

In New England settlers used square, flat-bottomed punts to hunt

▲ *An engraving from 1590 by Theodore de Bry shows natives in Virginia using fire to hollow out a log for a canoe. The man on the right fans the flames, and both of them scrape away the charred wood inside.*

waterbirds on the numerous ponds and lakes. In the winter runners on the bottoms allowed the punts to be used as sleds.

Pinnaces were the most common and versatile boats to ply the North American coastal waters. These small, fast sailing ships were used for everything from exploring to hauling trade goods. Their smaller size allowed them to push upstream to the fall lines. The first pinnace to be built in America was the *Virginia*, constructed in 1607 near the Kennebec River in Maine.

RIVER TRADING LINKS

As Americans pressed inland in the 18th century, they needed boats that would navigate the shallow, boulder-strewn rapids in the rivers above the fall lines. Long, shallow, flat-bottomed boats, called bateaux, were developed to take trade goods from the interior lands to the fall line and harbor cities. This river transportation encouraged the development of roads leading to and from boat-landing points.

The bateaux ranged in length from 20 ft (6 m) to 80 ft (24 m). The vessels usually traveled in convoys and were operated by several pole-wielding men who kept the bateaux headed in the right direction and off the rocks.

These were trade boats, loaded with such bulky items as tobacco, flour, iron, and cloth, not passenger boats.

The trip downstream was fast but dangerous. The trip upstream was hard, with the polemen pushing against the current, and inland portages, or journeys on foot carrying the boats, around rapids a necessity.

In Virginia the better-built bateaux that made the arduous return journey were called sharpies because they were tapered at each end to cut through the current. They were seven feet (2.1 m) wide and 70 feet (21.3 m)

▼ A flat-bottomed cargo-carrying boat heads down the Misssissipi River. The square front of the craft made it difficult to maneuver, and it required a large rudder at the stern.

long. A number of bateaux were rough-built, almost like giant rafts, and were not meant to last longer than a single voyage. Once the downstream destination was reached, these river boats were torn up and sold for lumber or firewood. Many houses in river cities were made from boat lumber. For the boatmen the return trip back upstream was made by wagon, on horseback, or on foot.

SEE ALSO

CRAFTS ■ ENVIRONMENT ■ FUR TRADE ■ IROQUOIS CONFEDERACY ■ MERCHANTS ■ MISSIONARIES ■ ROADS ■ TRADE

▲ *An 18th-century view of a canal in southwestern England. A horse could pull a much heavier load on water than on land.*

WASHINGTON'S POTOMAC CANAL

*G*eorge Washington was one of the first *Americans to explore the idea of canal development. He wanted to connect the Potomac River to the Ohio River and thus to the Mississippi River by constructing a long, straight canal, free from natural obstacles, running parallel to the river. There was already an extensive canal network in Britain at the time. Boats pulled by horses and mules that walked along a towpath at the canal bank were a vital part of the transport network. The canals that were eventually built in North America became a great asset to travelers and traders alike.*

Although he did not present this idea to the Virginia Legislature until 1772, Washington had thought about the idea since the 1740s, when he had surveyed the lands along the western reaches of the Potomac River. He had seen the terrible roads in what is now western Virginia, Maryland, and West Virginia but knew that the land there and farther west would be of great value. He sensed that a canal along the Potomac River could be the way to open up those lands. The Revolutionary War put a temporary halt to Washington's canal dream, but the idea was revived in 1784.

ROADS

By modern standards roads were primitive in colonial America. Travel was a slow and difficult process hampered by a network of narrow, dusty or muddy, rutted, and rocky roads. In the early years of European settlement in North America the majority of people rarely traveled farther from home than their church, their fields, or the courthouse. However, as the quality and number of roads began to improve, travel became faster in most areas.

Travelers and bulky shipments of goods alike might move over water where possible, across the hundreds of lakes and rivers, and along the thousands of miles of coastline.

Although most early European settlers lived near the waterways, as the number of colonists increased and land became scarcer, they were forced to settle in remote areas that were not accessible by boat. Water transport could also be costly and dangerous.

FROM PATHS TO ROADS

The earliest colonial roads often followed trails established by Native Americans or even by herds of animals. Unlike the Native Americans, who until Europeans arrived had not relied on horses for transport, settlers from the Old World often moved about by horse or carriage. Farmers transported grain to the mill or to

▼ *A colonist takes goods to the waterside in New England in about 1625. On the crudely surfaced roads of the time a sled was as useful as a wagon.*

R

market, and preachers traveled between communities spreading the Gospel.

Transport by pack animals (horses in eastern North America and mules in New Mexico) generally depended on some kind of path, as did transport by cart. Heavy, wheeled wagons and carriages, however, required wider, smoother roads than pack animals.

Public roads connected towns only if the local government had sufficient money, engineering skill, and available labor. In many areas no money changed hands for road construction and maintenance, since men were obliged to work several days each year on the roads. Sometimes they would use sand and gravel or else timbers placed together across the road. Longer roads tended to follow the contours of the landscape to avoid hills, ravines, rivers, and brooks.

LONG-HAUL HIGHWAYS

By the second half of the 18th century several long highways had come into existence in North America. In the Spanish colonies in the southwest the Camino Real (Royal

Highway), which extended from Mexico City to Santa Fe, was established around 1600. A wagon train could take six months to run the length of this road.

In the English colonies by the 1670s the Great Eastern Road connected Boston and New York. In 1766 a stagecoach service connecting New York and Philadelphia commenced, a distance of 100 miles (160 km) that could, if conditions were favorable, be covered in two days. By that time the Great Wagon Road reached south from Pennsylvania through the Shenandoah Valley and into the Carolinas.

SEE ALSO
RIVER TRAVEL

▲ *Toward the end of the colonial period the Conestoga wagon carrying settlers westward became a common sight.*

◄ *The Baltimore Road cuts through a New England landscape of cabins, fields, and woodland.*

ROANOKE SETTLEMENT

English America had its beginnings at Roanoke Island, located on the Outer Banks of North Carolina. In 1584 Elizabeth I gave Sir Walter Raleigh authority to explore and colonize the area of North America north of Spanish Florida.

Raleigh's first expedition set out that year. He reached Roanoke Island, selected it as a possible place for an English settlement, and named the entire Atlantic coast region "Virginia."

FIRST SETTLEMENTS

A second expedition, under Sir Richard Grenville, followed in 1585 with seven vessels and 600 men. When Grenville returned to England, he left behind 107 men under Ralph Lane to build houses and a fort on the island. They did so, but they also killed some of the local natives who refused to supply them with more food. In June of 1586 Lane and his men chose to leave America and return to England.

Soon after the departure of Lane and his men Grenville arrived with fresh supplies and a new group of colonists who found the place deserted. He left 15 men to hold the fort through the following winter, but they were attacked and killed by natives. By now Raleigh was losing enthusiasm for his scheme.

However, in 1587 he funded another attempt at settlement under John White. Three vessels carried 112 men, women, and children to the island. They rebuilt the fort, repaired the houses, and settled in at the "Citty of Ralegh." White's daughter, Eleanor Dare, had a daughter, Virginia Dare, the first child born in North America to English parents.

White left Roanoke Island to return to England for supplies and more settlers. However, he had to wait three years before making a return voyage. England had gone to war with Spain, and the Spanish captured White when he tried to return. He then had to wait for ships to become available at the end of the war. When he returned in 1590, he found the fort and houses deserted and the colonists nowhere to be seen.

SEE ALSO

DRAKE, SIR FRANCIS ■ NORTH CAROLINA ■ RALEIGH, SIR WALTER ■ VIRGINIA

▲ *Sir Richard Grenville took the first English colonists to Roanoke Island in 1585.*

◄ *Sir Walter Raleigh (center) on Roanoke Island, which he selected as a suitable location for the first English settlement in America.*

ST. AUGUSTINE

The first permanent European settlement in North America, St. Augustine is located in north Florida. The first landing was by the Spanish navigator Juan Ponce de León in April 1513, but it was his fellow countryman Pedro Menéndez de Avilés who founded St. Augustine in 1565. He marched his men overland and destroyed Fort Caroline, which had been established in 1564 by French Huguenots (Protestants) a short distance to the north.

FORTIFIED SETTLEMENT

On June 7, 1585, a raiding party led by the English privateer Sir Francis Drake almost destroyed the settlement. Although it was rebuilt, St. Augustine never really flourished. Throughout the next 200 years the Spanish government showed more interest in exploiting the wealth of Central and South America and viewed St. Augustine, the northernmost outpost of the Spanish American empire, as a defensive station against the encroachment of the French and the British. In 1672 the stone-walled Castillo de San Marcos was built in the town. It is the oldest fort still standing in North America.

In 1739 the Spanish authorities in St. Augustine offered sanctuary to slaves who had escaped from plantations in South Carolina during a slave uprising known as the Stono Rebellion.

Throughout the early 18th century the Spanish colonists in Florida spent much of the time warring with the British colonists in neighboring Georgia. In 1740 Governor James Oglethorpe led a force of 2,000 men to St. Augustine but failed to conquer the heavily fortified settlement.

The town remained in Spanish hands until the end of the French and Indian War (1754–1763), when it was ceded by treaty to Britain. During the Revolutionary War St. Augustine served as a haven for Loyalists from the northern colonies but was ceded back to Spain in the Treaty of Paris (1783) along with the rest of Florida.

SEE ALSO

FLORIDA ■ FREE BLACKS ■ FRENCH AND INDIAN WAR ■ NEW SPAIN ■ PONCE DE LEÓN, JUAN ■ STONO REBELLION ■ TREATY OF PARIS, 1783

▼ *This overhead view of the fort at St. Augustine is taken from a Spanish map produced in 1577. The cannons that helped the fort repel the invaders from Georgia in 1740 can be clearly seen.*

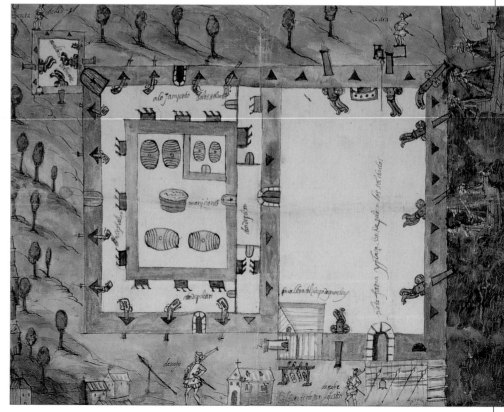

SALEM WITCH TRIALS

In 1692 in the small village of Salem, Massachusetts, there occurred some of the strangest events in the whole of American colonial history. These events became known as the Salem Witch Trials.

In the course of eight months, in Salem and a number of surrounding villages, over 100 people were accused of witchcraft. Fifty of them "confessed," 26 were found guilty by trial and jury, and 19 were put to death. Children had seizures, went into trances, and claimed their own parents were witches. The bodies of the accused were closely examined for "marks of Satan," and wild accounts were given of wandering ghosts and evil black cats.

WITCHCRAFT TRADITION

Prosecutions for witchcraft had always been a feature of the Christian

▲ *Pointing fingers identify a supposed witch in the Salem courtroom.*

◄ *The title page of a pamphlet written by Cotton Mather and published in Boston in 1693.*

religion. However, the more rigorous branches of the Protestant faith, such as Puritanism, were even more fearful of "the devil's work." They believed that a person could not only be possessed by Satan, but that he or she could cast spells and that possessed women could give birth to his children. People found guilty of witchcraft might be sentenced to be burned, hanged, drowned, or crushed to death—though they might avoid the death penalty if they confessed.

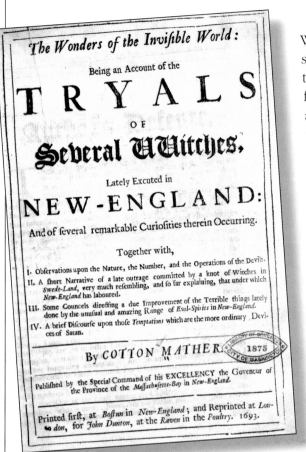

The title page of Cotton Mather's own account of the Salem Witch Trials, published in Boston in 1693.

The governor of Massachusetts, Sir William Phips, decided to appoint a special court to try the cases. There the accusers often screamed and fainted when face-to-face with the accused, claiming that they had seen them walking the town by night in the shape of "specters." For their part, the accused found it hard to defend themselves. They were told that the absence of "marks of Satan" on their bodies simply showed how cunning the devil was. And when some of them were found innocent, the judge instructed the jury to "think again" —in other words, to change its verdict.

Many of the accused therefore "confessed" rather than face a guilty verdict and possible death sentence. Unfortunately, in their confession they also had to name people who had helped them "do the devil's work."

This 17th-century house, which has been restored, in Salem, Massachusetts, was the home of one of the Witch Trial judges.

FIRST ACCUSATIONS

The first signs that there was something sinister in Salem occurred in February 1692, when the daughter and the niece of Samuel Parris, the village minister, began having fits that doctors in the town described as "bewitchment." The proof of this, they said, was that the two girls were friends with the Parris's slave girl, Tituba, who admitted using charms to foretell the future.

Soon other young girls began having seizures, blaming not only Tituba but also two respectable widows, Sarah Osburn and Sarah Good. By May more than 25 people had been accused, including several men and a former minister of Salem, George Burroughs.

TRIAL AND PUNISHMENT

As the weeks went by, the village of Salem was torn apart by accusations and counteraccusations. By June the trouble had also spread to the neighboring villages of Andover, Haverhill, Topsfield, and Gloucester. One by one the supposedly guilty were sent to a horrible death. Giles Corey was among the victims. His wife had already been executed, but when Corey himself was brought to trial, he refused to speak—because even if he confessed, he knew his lands would be confiscated. His silence did him no good: he was ordered to be crushed beneath a pile of stones until he spoke.

By the fall that year some church ministers at last began to be concerned about the so-called evidence against the accused. However, action was taken only when the accusers turned on the wives of

▲ This engraving of the trial of George Jacobs, one of the men accused of witchcraft, conveys some of the hysteria that surrounded the Salem trials.

eminent men in the district, including that of the governor himself. Then even Samuel Parris, who had been most determined to hunt down those who had "bewitched" his girls, began to think better of the trials—while the judge himself now publicly expressed his doubts about the accusers. By early 1693 the court refused to hear any more charges of witchcraft. However, it was not until 1711 that any compensation was paid to the surviving victims.

RATIONAL EXPLANATIONS

Many reasons have been given to explain this extraordinary episode. One is that the "bewitched" children, brought up in a strict Puritan manner,

S

SARAH CARRIER'S CONFESSION

SARAH CARRIER, AGED SEVEN, WAS ACCUSED OF BEING A WITCH IN AUGUST 1692. HER MOTHER HAD ALREADY BEEN CONDEMNED TO DEATH WHEN THE LITTLE GIRL WAS BROUGHT BEFORE THE MAGISTRATES. HERE IS AN EXTRACT FROM HER CONFESSION:

Magistrates: How long hast thou been a witch?

Answer: Ever since I was six years old...

Question: Who made you witch?

Answer: My mother, she made me set my hand to a book [of the devil]...

[Being asked who else was there, she answered her Aunt and her cousin.]

Question: What did they promise to give you?

Answer: A black dog.

Question: Did the dog ever come to you?

Answer: No.

Question: But you say you saw a black cat once. What did it say to you?

Answer: It said it would tear me in pieces if I did not set my hand to the book...

Question: How did you afflict folks?

Answer: I pinched them.

[Being asked whether she went in her body or spirit, she said in her spirit. And she said that her mother carried her thither to afflict.]

Question: How did your mother carry you when she was in prison?

Answer: She came like a black cat.

Question: How did you know it was your mother?

Answer: The cat told me so that she was my mother.

wanted to attract attention and even to get their revenge on their parents. Another view is that it was a case of persecution of the weaker members of society (most of the accused were women or poor people) or of those who did not abide by its rules. A third explanation is that the fiercest accusations came from young girls affected by physical and mental changes as they approached puberty. Lastly, it has been suggested that the trials were the result of personal grudges. Salem had a history of conflict between neighbors; accusing someone of witchcraft was a good way to get even in such a religious society.

OBSESSIVE BELIEF

However, it is most likely that a combination of these reasons led to the trials. The Puritan obsession with sin and strong belief in the devil created the perfect conditions for charges of witchcraft. It must also be remembered that Massachusetts had just gone through a period of upheaval, beginning with King Philip's War and ending in war with New France. These misfortunes weakened the government and made people look for someone to blame.

END OF WITCHCRAFT

The Salem trials marked the passing of an era. Massachusetts and the other English colonies were slowly becoming more worldly—their institutions less and less influenced by the church. Even at the time Salem was seen as an example of the terrible things that can happen when religious beliefs are allowed to influence law. After 1700 there were no more witchcraft trials in the colonies.

SEE ALSO

MASSACHUSETTS ■ MATHER, COTTON ■ RELIGION, PURITAN ■ SUPERNATURAL

SANTA FE

The town of Santa Fe was founded in 1610—just three years after the Jamestown colony—as the capital of the recently declared Spanish royal province of New Mexico. It was originally named Villa Real de la Santa Fe de San Francisco de Asis, or the Royal City of the Holy Faith of St. Francis of Assisi. This name reflected the important missionary role of the Franciscan monks who were among the first to settle there. It was soon shortened to Santa Fe.

SEAT OF GOVERNMENT

The governor of New Mexico, Don Pedro de Peralta, who replaced Juan de Onate in 1609, was involved in planning the city, which was built on the site of a pueblo inhabited by

Native Americans of the Tewa tribe. It followed the Spanish pattern of siting the main buildings around a large central plaza. The actual construction work was done by Native Americans as part of a forced labor scheme called *repartimiento de indios*.

Santa Fe was the first seat of government to be established in the North American colonies and was settled by 250 Spanish colonists and 700 servants. Most of these servants were Mexicans of the Tlaxcalan tribe who had accompanied their masters on the journey north.

While the Spanish lived in houses around the plaza, the servants created a community of their own on a hill south of the Santa Fe River. The church of San Miguel, the oldest

▲ *The Palace of the Governors in Santa Fe was the regional seat of government for New Mexico from 1610 until 1909.*

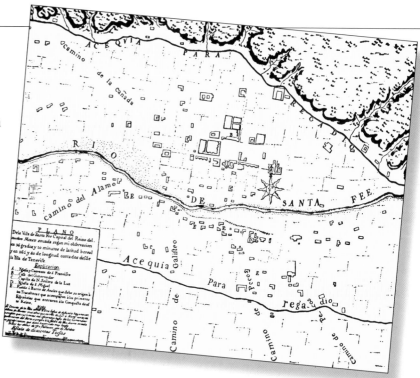

church surviving in the United States, was built for their use. The city did not grow very quickly. The population had barely doubled by August 1680, when a force of 2,000 Pueblo and Apache, many with Spanish weapons and armor, attacked the city as part of a general rebellion known as the Pueblo Revolt.

The colonists were gradually forced back into the government buildings as their houses burned. The governor, Antonio de Otermin, surrendered the city on September 21 and was allowed to lead the surviving colonists south to sanctuary in the town of El Paso, which is now Cuidad Juarez in Mexico.

BATTLING FOR SANTA FE

The city was then occupied by the Tewa and Tanos tribes for 13 years, until it was stormed by the new governor, Don Diego de Vargas, in 1693. Seventy Pueblos who had refused to surrender were executed for treason. Vargas then made the city the base for his largely successful campaign to bring the pueblos back under Spanish rule. In the 18th century Santa Fe was established as the administrative center of New Mexico and the base for expeditions into the interior of the continent. It was also a missionary and military center, although its presidio, or frontier fort, had a permanent garrison of fewer than 100 men.

The town never grew very large; its population in 1765 was just 2,324. Trading was difficult, since the only outlet for goods was Mexico, where the merchants of Chihuahua controlled the market to their own advantage. In the late 18th century trading routes were opened to San Antonio and Tucson.

The Palace of the Governors, a long, single-story adobe building constructed by Peralta in 1610, still stands on the north side of the Plaza. It was restored in 1914.

SEE ALSO

NEW MEXICO ■ NEW SPAIN ■ ONATE, JUAN DE

▲ *The earliest known map of Santa Fe, made by José de Urratia in about 1767, shows the main buildings of the town on the north bank of the Santa Fe River.*

▼ *The town of Santa Fe (in the midbackground) is situated on the broad lowlands of the Rio Grande Valley.*

BATTLE OF SARATOGA

The American victory at the Battle of Saratoga in October 1777 marked the turning point of the Revolutionary War. The British suffered a major defeat, surrendering 5,700 troops to American forces. The American victory also convinced France, Spain, and the Netherlands to formally enter the war. This diverted British forces to the Caribbean, where French and Spanish attacks on British colonial possessions seemed likely.

THE BRITISH ADVANCE

In early 1777 General Burgoyne and Lord Germain planned a strategy to isolate New England from the rest of the colonies. Burgoyne would march the main part of his army south from Montreal, while another force would march eastward from Fort Oswego on Lake Ontario. General Howe's army in the south would march northward, and all three forces would converge at Albany, New York. The strategy might have worked, but Howe decided to move against Philadelphia instead. Washington moved elements of the Continental Army south to counter Howe's move against Philadelphia and also sent forces north against Burgoyne.

Initially, Burgoyne's army of 8,000 troops advanced steadily into New York. Heavily outnumbered, the American commander, General Philip Schuyler, decided to abandon Fort Ticonderoga and concentrate on delaying tactics in the dense woodland of upper New York. The loss of Fort Ticonderoga angered the Continental Congress, which replaced Schuyler with General Horatio Gates.

▲ *General Benedict Arnold (seated at center) was wounded in an attack on a Hessian position during the Battle of Saratoga.*

◄ *Watched by officers of the Continental Army and militia, General Burgoyne (in red jacket followed by an aide) offers his sword in surrender to General Gates (at center).*

However, Schuyler's tactics slowed Burgoyne's army and allowed time for American reinforcements to arrive. By August supply problems gripped the British, and in western New York the British advance from Fort Oswego was halted by General Benedict Arnold. Burgoyne's three-pronged attack on Albany had been reduced to one.

THE BRITISH DEFEAT

By September 1777 the Patriot forces under Gates had grown to 7,000. The remaining British forces amounted to only 6,000, yet Burgoyne remained confident and crossed the Hudson River just north of Saratoga on September 13–14. Gates fortified his position 10 miles (16 km) south of Saratoga and 24 miles (38 km) north of Albany. On September 19 Burgoyne engaged the American line. In the ensuing battle at Freeman's Farm the Americans outnumbered their opponents, but superior British and German discipline prevented an American victory. Burgoyne's force retreated and fortified a position one mile from the Americans. The British losses numbered 600 casualties and prisoners, while the Americans suffered 300 casualties.

On September 21 Burgoyne received a message that British Lieutenant General Sir Henry Clinton, now in command at New York City, had sent 2,000 troops north to divert Gates's army. Burgoyne decided to wait for Clinton's arrival, but American raids diminished his supplies and encouraged Loyalists to desert. While the British force dwindled, General Benjamin Lincoln's reinforcements swelled the Patriot forces to almost 11,000. On October 7 Burgoyne sent 1,500 troops toward the American right flank to determine whether he should attack or hold. The American counterattacked at Bemis Heights.

British losses of nearly 600 were three times those of the Patriots. With no aid from Clinton in sight Burgoyne retreated north, reaching Saratoga on October 10. Gates's main force, now numbering 17,000, followed, while Brigadier General John Stark's 1,100 strong militia force crossed the Hudson River cutting off Burgoyne's retreat. On October 14 Burgoyne sent a letter to Gates asking for terms of surrender. Hopeful that Clinton might still arrive, Burgoyne delayed before finally surrendering on October 17.

SEE ALSO
AMERICAN REVOLUTIONARY WAR ■ ARNOLD, BENEDICT ■ BURGOYNE, GENERAL JOHN ■ HESSSIANS ■ WASHINGTON, GEORGE

▼ *General Horatio Gates watches redcoat prisoners march off into captivity following his victory at the Battle of Saratoga.*

SCHOOLS AND COLLEGES

Education in colonial America was recognized as a vital part of a young person's training in life, but each colony maintained a separate approach to teaching its younger generation. Education was not generally a matter of colonial government policy and action. As in early 17th-century England, there was no government-run system of schools, colleges, and universities. Education was usually provided by the members of a child's family or a tutor employed by them, or else by the church or town authorities.

The founding fathers of the New England colonies such as Plymouth, Massachusetts Bay, Connecticut, and Rhode Island were from various branches of the Protestant religion. These groups stressed the importance of each individual's ability to read the Bible. They usually settled in close-knit communities and founded village schools soon after they settled.

At a town meeting the local householders would vote "to procure a suitable schoolmaster, to teach children to Read, Write, and Sipher." Sipher was the term used in the

▲ *This illustration shows a "Dame" school. This was a school run by a schoolmistress in her home in early 18th-century New England. The boy on the left is being punished by standing with his back to the class wearing a paper hat known as a "dunce's cap."*

British colonies to refer to the process of doing arithmetic.

FIRST TEACHERS

The first schoolmaster was teaching in Boston in 1635. Charleston hired a teacher in 1636, and Dorchester in 1639. The Massachusetts School Act of 1647 required every town of 50 families to maintain a schoolmaster or else be fined. In reality many of the poorer towns chose to pay the fine. The act also required every town of 100 families to maintain a grammar school to teach Latin and Greek. This meant that a high school education was supposedly available at public expense.

LITERACY LEVELS

The New England colonies were very successful in teaching basic literacy. In England about 50 percent of males were literate in the 18th century. The rate was much higher in the New England colonies. There, about 90 percent of males could read the printed word and sign their names in the 18th century. The rate of literacy for New England females was lower. Some 50 to 60 percent of women seem to have been literate and able to sign their names. Many colonial Americans could read printed material but had not received enough formal education to read handwriting or to write much more than their own names. If they needed a letter written, they often asked their minister to do it for them.

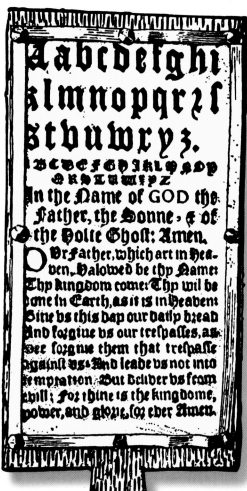

▲ The alphabet and the Lord's Prayer were mounted on a wooden board called a horn.

▶ This page is from Benjamin Harris's "New England Primer." First published around 1690, it was the only school textbook in early colonial America.

SOUTHERN COLONIES

In southern colonies such as Virginia, Maryland, and the Carolinas the education of children was more difficult. The population was scattered around the countryside on farms and plantations, making it difficult to get children together for lessons.

Rich planter families were also reluctant to send their children to school with the poor. Many hired private tutors for their children, and there were fewer public schools as a result. In Virginia, Maryland, and the Carolinas many of those tutors were young men from Britain who had recently graduated from university and decided to seek their fortune in America. Private tutors often also taught the female children.

For many girls in the British colonies the main part of their education was learning to sew, do

A | In Adam's Fall We sinned all.

B | Thy Life to mend, This Book attend.

C | The Cat doth play, And after slay.

D | A Dog will bite A Thief at night.

E | An Eagle's flight Is out of sight.

F | The idle Fool Is whipt at school.

GERMAN TEACHING

In the British North American colonies the largest group of non-English-speaking settlers were German-speakers from the Rhineland and Switzerland. They settled in Pennsylvania beginning about 1690 because William Penn's agents made special efforts to attract them. His colony offered freedom of religion to all Christian denominations. These settlers were a mixture of Lutherans, Reformed, Moravians, Mennonites, Brethren, and Baptists.

Each group undertook the education of its own children, keeping the German language alive. Within some of these denominations church ministers operated schools, while in other denominations children were educated at home. The Germans set up printing presses so that they could produce their own German-language texts. German settlers moved into the Valley of Virginia in the 1730s, and Moravians made two important town settlements in North Carolina.

▼ *Colonial classrooms were often cramped and sparsely furnished. Children of all ages were taught together.*

handwork, cook, and manage a household. The daughters of wealthier families often attended classes with a dancing master and a musician.

CHURCH SCHOOLS

In all of the British North American colonies ministers often ran schools in their own homes. These schools were usually called academies after the Greek word for a house of learning. Thomas Jefferson and James Madison, the third and fourth presidents of the United States, received their basic education at academies run by ministers of the established church in Virginia. In Pennsylvania, Delaware, New Jersey, and the western part of

▲ *By the mid-18th century Harvard College, first established as a training college for the clergy in 1636, was teaching a wide variety of subjects.*

Virginia Presbyterian ministers usually kept such an academy. One of the first in western Virginia was Augusta Academy, which Presbyterian settlers founded about 1750.

Sometimes the children of very poor persons and illegitimate children received a better education than the children of middling, small-farm families. In colonies with an established church the men who governed the parish or congregation had to see that orphan and illegitimate children were "bound out" for training and education at public expense. Those children became indentured servants when they were old enough to work. Terms of the indenture required the master to teach them to read and write, and to train them to

NEW FRANCE

*I*n French-settled Quebec education of children and young persons was largely in the hands of the Roman Catholic Church and the parents of the children. Often the local parish priests would teach the sons of some of the farmers in the parish. The Ursuline order of nuns arrived in New France around 1640. In Quebec City on the St. Lawrence River they founded the Ursuline Convent in 1641. The school at the convent educated young girls in reading, writing, the catechism, and needlework. In 1663 the first bishop of Quebec, Francois de Montmorency Laval, founded a seminary for the training of priests. This institution grew over the years and later became Laval University. Even after the British took control of Quebec with the Treaty of Paris in 1763, the majority of the residents remained French-speaking, and they continued their own schools.*

HIGHER EDUCATION

The early English settlers moved quickly to create opportunities for higher education. This meant that young men entering the ministry and the educated professions would not have to cross the Atlantic to attend an English or Scottish university. In 1636, just six years after Puritans began to settle in Massachusetts Bay, they founded Harvard College.

Six more colleges, some of which are still functioning today, were founded in colonial America before the Revolutionary War. Most were established by branches of the Protestant Church, and all were in the northern colonies. Princeton (Presbyterian, 1746) and Rutgers (Dutch Reformed, 1766) were in New Jersey; Columbia University in New York City (Anglican, 1754); Brown (Baptist, 1764) was in Providence, Rhode Island. New England Congregationalists founded Yale in New Haven, Connecticut, in 1701,

be self-supporting when the term of the indenture had been worked out. This usually meant teaching the boys a trade or farming skills and training the girls in housekeeping.

In the colonial period slavery was permitted in all the North American colonies. African-American and Native-American slave children rarely had the opportunity for an education, except for that provided by their elders. Some southern British colonies had laws forbidding the teaching of reading and writing to slaves.

▲ *The Wren building at the College of William and Mary in Wiliamsburg, Virginia.*

▶ *James Blair (1656-1743) founded the College of William and Mary in 1693.*

S along with Dartmouth in New Hampshire, which had a strong interest in Native-American education.

Most of these small colleges taught subjects such as Latin, Greek, Hebrew, rhetoric, logic, mathematics, physics, moral philosophy, and theology.

The first effort to found a college in Virginia in the 1620s failed. It was not until 1693 that the College of William and Mary opened its doors in Williamsburg. An important part of this college in the early years was its Indian School. Before and after the founding of William and Mary many of the wealthiest Virginia and Carolina planters sent their sons to England for a university education at either Oxford or Cambridge.

The University of Pennsylvania, chartered in Philadelphia in 1755, was the only school that was not tied to a church. Its trustees included Anglicans, Presbyterians, and Quakers. In 1775 and 1776 Presbyterians in

▲ *John Witherspoon (1723-1794), was a Scottish minister who served as president of the College of New Jersey, which later became Princeton College.*

Virginia founded two more schools that later became colleges, Liberty Hall Academy (Washington College) and Prince Edward Academy (Hampden-Sydney College). As a result of the creation of so many colleges, colonists had greater access to higher education than British people.

Nowhere in the colonies was higher education available to young women. While two of the colonial colleges made provision for education of Native Americans, very few from the many tribes ever attended. There was also no provision for any higher education for African Americans. In all, fewer than 10,000 young men received any higher education in the colleges of the British North American colonies. A primary or elementary school was the extent of most colonists' education.

SEE ALSO

CHILDREN ■ HARVARD COLLEGE ■ RELIGION, PURITAN ■ SLAVE CULTURE ■ WOMEN'S ROLES

▶ *A notice placed in the Virginia Gazette in November 1752 advertising the teaching services of Mr. John Walker and his wife, who had emigrated from London.*

JOHN WALKER,

LATELY arriv'd in *Williamsburg* from *London,* and who for ten Years paſt has been engag'd in the Education of Youth, undertakes to inſtruct young Gentlemen in Reading, Writing, Arithmetick, the moſt material Branches of Claſſical Learning, and ancient and modern Geography and Hiſtory; but, as the nobleſt End of Erudition and Human Attainments, he will exert his principal Endeavours to improve their Morals, in Proportion to their Progreſs in Learning, that no Parent may repent his Choice in truſting him with the Education of his Children.

Mrs. *Walker,* likewiſe, teaches young Ladies all Kinds of Needle Work; makes Capuchins, Shades, Hats, and Bonnets; and will endeavour to give Satisfaction to thoſe who ſhall honour her with their Cuſtom.

The above-mentioned *John Walker,* and his Wife, live at Mr. *Cobb's* new Houſe, next to Mr. *Coke's,* near the Road going down to the Capitol Landing; where there is alſo to be ſold, Mens Shoes and Pumps, *Turkey* Coffee, Edging and Lace for Ladies Caps, and ſome Gold Rings.

SCIENCE

The first European settlers in North America were far removed, but not completely isolated, from European developments in scientific thought. In time many settlers brought with them a variety of specializations and interests that were further stimulated by the fascinating wildlife and landscape of America, and much pioneering scientific research and development of scientific theory was carried out by American colonists. Centers of learning that later taught subjects such as astronomy, physics, and botany were founded at Harvard College in 1636 and at the College of William and Mary, Williamsburg, Virginia, in 1693.

However, it was not until the 18th century that science in the colonies began to develop its distinctive and impressive approach, with an emphasis on the practical side of science. Many of the American scientists who became celebrated for their work had little formal education but in later life were recognized for the importance of their work at home and abroad.

JOHN BARTRAM AND SON

One of the most remarkable of such men was John Bartram. Bartram was born in Darby, Pennsylvania, in 1699 and developed an interest in plants and animals while growing up on his uncle's farm. He got his own farm near Philadelphia in 1728 and set up a botanical garden at Kingsessing. He exchanged information with the famous Swedish botanist Carl Linnaeus and in 1743 set out on an expedition to explore the fabulous flora of North America right up to the southern shores of Lake Ontario. As well as

identifying many species, Bartram was the first person to experiment with cross-breeding plants in North America. His garden at Kingsessing soon became world famous. On some of his later explorations he was joined by his son William Bartram, whose sketches and collection of plants and their seeds were of great significance in their own right. The lives of Native Americans were considered to be a worthy subject of study, and both the

▼ *William Bartram, the son of the famous botanist John Bartram, was a talented artist and made countless drawings of the plants he found during explorations.*

▶ *Franklin flew a kite during a thunderstorm in 1752 to investigate the properties of lightning flashes.*

▼ *Franklin's apparatus for generating static electricity, as depicted in his book* Experiments and Observations on Electricity.

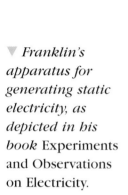

Bartrams made some valuable records of the lives of native peoples.

BENJAMIN FRANKLIN

Bartram became a friend of the most celebrated of all colonial American scientists, Benjamin Franklin, and was a founder member of the highly influential American Philosophical Society that was established in 1744. Most of the significant scientists of the day belonged to the society, which had grown out of the Leather Apron Club, or Junto, which Franklin formed in 1727 to debate all kinds of issues, including scientific theories. In 1751 Franklin also set up the Academy of Philadelphia, which formed the basis of the University of Pennsylvania, a center for scientific learning. Franklin invented the lightning rod and much of the terminology that is still used to describe electricity (such as positive and negative). He also designed an iron stove that was much more energy-efficient than the open grate type popular at the time. Bifocal lenses were another of Franklin's ingenious ideas.

Many of the scientists of the day developed their interests while learning a trade. After Franklin finished his education at the age of 10, he was apprenticed to his brother, James, who owned a printing plant. He later established his own printers in Philadelphia and in the 1740s developed a fascination with electricity after an English friend sent him a device that generated electricity.

Along with other scientifically minded tradesmen such as the silversmith Philip Syng Jr., Franklin conducted a series of experiments into atmospheric electricity. In one famous experiment he flew a kite in a violent thunderstorm to demonstrate that lightning was electricity in the atmosphere and came up with the idea of putting a conducting rod on the tops of buildings to protect them from damage. The results were sent to London, where they were highly acclaimed and brought European recognition for him and his colleagues. Franklin was a great believer in the practical application of science to common problems and was extremely frustrated when one of his experiments into static electricity was adapted into a parlor game.

ASTRONOMY

Another notable tradesman-scientist who was elected to the American Philosophical Society in 1768 was David Rittenhouse, a clockmaker with a special interest in astronomy. Before the age of electronics precision clockwork mechanisms were important for all kinds of scientific and mathematical calculations, and had a vital part to play in calculating the movement of stars and planets across the night sky.

▼ *One of Franklin's experiments into static electricity was turned into a parlor game.*

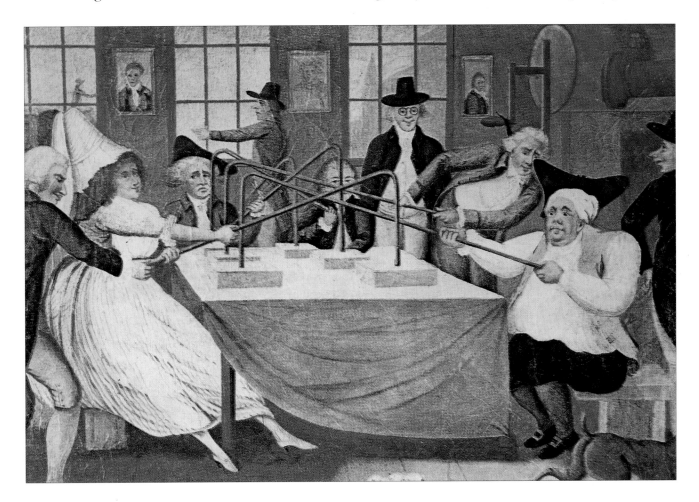

S

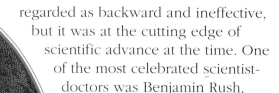

▶ *David Rittenhouse (1732–1796) sitting next to the telescope with which he made his greatest discovery, the atmosphere of Venus.*

▼ *The physician Benjamin Rush (1745–1813) served as surgeon general in the Continental Army during the Revolutionary War.*

Rittenhouse used his talents to make the first orrery (a mechanical model of the solar system) in colonial America and also built the first telescope in the colonies. With this device he made observations of the path of Venus crossing the Sun that enabled him to conclude that Venus had an atmosphere. Rittenhouse was elected a member of the Royal Society in London in 1795. Among other notable astronomers was John Winthrop, a Harvard professor who measured the earth's distance from the Sun to an accuracy of 98 percent. Both astronomy and clockmaking had great practical benefits for sailors and explorers, who could use stars and clocks to navigate.

MEDICINE

In the field of medicine the colonial approach to healing would now be regarded as backward and ineffective, but it was at the cutting edge of scientific advance at the time. One of the most celebrated scientist-doctors was Benjamin Rush, who had studied first at the College of New Jersey, Princeton, and then in Europe. He returned to become professor of chemistry at the College of Philadelphia and to give immensely popular public lectures based on his theory that all disease was caused by "overstimulation" of the blood vessels. Rush believed that many ailments could be cured by blood-letting—a common medical practice—which involved draining some of the patient's blood. He also wrote the first American book on diseases of the mind—*Medical Inquiries and Observations upon the Diseases of the Mind*—which he believed mostly had physical causes. He become so confident of his abilities that he criticized the running of military hospitals in the Revolutionary War and fell out of favor with George Washington.

In the late 18th century correspondence across the Atlantic was still slow, but the development of science in colonial America was not isolated from that in Europe, and there were lively exchanges of theories and information. What distinguished much of scientific discovery and endeavor in colonial America was the application of new discoveries and theories to practical problems by men who had a background in trade and technology.

SEE ALSO

BOOKS AND LIBRARIES ▪ DISEASE ▪ FRANKLIN, BENJAMIN ▪ HARVARD COLLEGE ▪ MEDICINE ▪ SCHOOLS AND COLLEGES

JUNIPERO SERRA

Father Junipero Serra was born on the Spanish island of Majorca in the Mediterranean in 1713. He entered the Franciscan order in 1730, eventually earning a doctorate in theology. He was sent to Mexico City in 1749, from where he served in various Spanish missions in Mexico. He was also the founder of many of the early Spanish missions in Alta (Upper) California.

SPANISH MISSIONS

California was hard to reach by foot from the Spanish presidios (forts) in northern Mexico. The harbors at San Diego and Monterey were known to exist but had not been explored extensively. The Spanish appetite for conquest did not extend to California until Russian fur traders began exploring the California coast during the mid-18th century.

Father Serra established the Mission of San Diego de Alcala on July 16, 1769, after riding a mule 750 miles (1,207 km) up the Baja Peninsula to San Diego harbor. The other missions established by Father Serra were: San Carlos de Borromeo (1770); San Antonio de Padua (1771); San Gabriel (1771); San Luis Obispo (1772); San Francisco (1776); San Juan Capistrano (1776); Santa Clara (1777); and San Buenaventura (1782).

Father Serra was a deeply religious man whose skill as an administrator kept the missions prospering in the face of hostile Native Americans, disease, and starvation.

OFFICIAL RECOGNITION

Father Junipero Serra died on August 28, 1784, at the Mission of San Carlos de Borromeo. His piety and success in establishing the Catholic faith in California were recognized by the pope in the 1980s, when his special status was officially acknowledged.

SEE ALSO

CALIFORNIA ■ MISSIONARIES ■ NEW MEXICO ■ NEW SPAIN ■ RELIGION, CATHOLIC

▲ *Father Serra encouraged Spanish soldiers in California to intermarry with Native-American women, but few did so.*

S SHAWNEE

An ancient native historical record known as the Walum Olum records the split of the Shawnee from the Delaware tribe in about the year 1000. They traveled south and settled in territory straddling the Ohio River. At the end of the 18th century they were forced to migrate west by European settlers.

SHAWNEE GOVERNMENT

There were five distinct divisions among the Shawnee; the Chalagotha, Thawegila, Peckuwe, Kispoko, and Makujay. All of these divisions were ruled by a democratic tribal council composed of the divisional leaders, with an overall chief at its head. The tribal chief of the Shawnee was chosen from the ranks of the Chalagotha and Thawegila, and he was advised by a Grand Sachem, a tribal elder of great wisdom and experience. Another important figure was the tribal matriarch, a respected female elder who conveyed the views of the women of the tribe to the tribal chief.

The Peckuwe division had responsiblity for all religious matters within the tribe, and the Kispoko attended to all military matters. The Makujay provided the medicine men. All the divisons held regular councils that involved the senior and most respected male and female members.

Within these divisions were various clans. Clan membership was passed on by the father. Chiefs were chosen on a hereditary system through the clans, but Shawnee war chiefs were selected from among the bravest and most experienced warriors. They were related to the central Algonquian language group, which includes the

Sauk, Fox, Chippewa, Potawatomi, Ottawa, Menominee, Illinois, and Kickapoo tribes. The Shawnee formed alliances with some of these groups, primarily to defend their lands.

SUMMER AND WINTER

In spring and summer the Shawnee clans gathered in river valleys in large villages made up of pole-framed family wigwams covered with birch or elm bark. Each village had a larger council house (also made of poles and bark) where the council debated and religious ceremonies took place. In nearby crop fields the women grew corn, pumpkins, squashes, and beans.

In the fall, once the harvest was in, the village broke up into smaller family groups that went to live in hunting camps in the woods, perhaps a single isolated bark lodge. Here the men hunted, trapped, and fished, while the women gathered fruit and nuts and prepared animal skins.

▲ *Kish-Kal-Wa, a Shawnee chief, is shown wearing the traditional nose ring of Shawnee warriors.*

EXILE AND RESETTLEMENT

In the 17th century the Shawnee were driven out of their home in the center of the Ohio Valley by the Iroquois, who were attempting to take over the trade in beaver skins. They became widely scattered. Some went west to what is now Illinois, while others settled in the Cumberland Valley. Another group went much further south and became part of the Creek Confederacy.

In the 1720s the northern groups, and some of the Shawnee from the south, returned to their ancestral homelands on the Ohio—territory that had been claimed by Pennsylvania.

The Shawnee were willing to ally with just about any tribe to protect the land they had reclaimed.

◄ *A Shawnee warrior in the early 19th century. By this time most of his tribe had abandoned their lands in the Ohio Valley.*

▼ *A British military map of 1764 showing "Indian Country" in that part of the Ohio Valley inhabited by the Shawnee.*

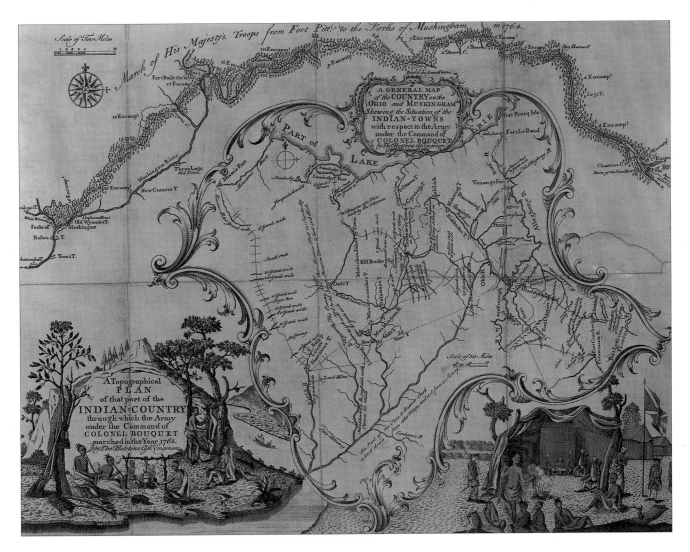

WIGWAMS

THE SHAWNEE CLANS USED A DIFFERENT TYPE OF WIGWAM IN THE SPRING AND SUMMER, AND WINTER MONTHS.

▶ *The winter wigwam was constructed in a dome shape by bending the ends of 10-15 ft (3-4.5 m) long saplings that were secured in the ground into a U-shape. Sheets of elm bark covered the frame.*

▶ *The summer and spring wigwam was made by laying straight branches or saplings about 10-11 ft (3-3.35 m) long in a cone shape. The frame was then covered with elm bark (or birch bark north of Ohio). The bark was first stripped from the tree in sheets and then laid on the ground to dry.*

Shawnee families built their winter wigwams in solitary woodland hunting encampments.
In summer they lived in larger groups along the river valleys.

CLASHES WITH EUROPEANS

During the 1730s tensions between the Shawnee and frontier settlers began to erupt into violent clashes. The pressures on hunting land in the Ohio Valley were further increased by an influx of people from the Delaware tribe, who had been displaced from their lands in eastern Pennsylvania by European settlers.

The Shawnee and Delaware took revenge on the Pennsylvanians in the French and Indian War (1754–1763). Initially they remained neutral, hoping that the Quaker assembly in Philadelphia would return their lands.

In 1755, however, when British regiments under Braddock were defeated by a French and native force in the Ohio Valley, the Shawnee and Delaware became allies of the French in return for weapons. War parties attacked settlements up and down the frontier. They were merciless, sparing only the few Quakers they found. The frontier was depopulated and pushed back by as much as 50 miles (80 km) as refugees abandoned their homes and poured into the eastern counties of Pennsylvania. The Native-American allies also made attacks on Virginia but met sterner resistance from a militia regiment led by Colonel George Washington.

The British victories in 1759 and 1760, coupled with their promise to withdraw east of the Allegheny Mountains if they were victorious, persuaded the Shawnee and their native allies to switch sides. When the British achieved overall victory at the end of the war, they simply failed to keep the promises they had made.

The Shawnee fought the British again in the 1763 rebellion led by Pontiac but again had no lasting success, and the threat to their territory continued. In 1774 a southern Shawnee warrior named Cornstalk led warriors from a league of western tribes to attack European settlements in Kentucky. They had some initial successes but were eventually beaten, and again the Shawnee were forced north of the Ohio River.

After the Revolutionary War broke out, the southern Shawnee, allied with Iroquois, Delaware, Ottawa, and Cherokee, attacked American frontier settlements in the south. In 1778 the Kentucky militia made several reprisal raids on Shawnee settlements in Ohio, destroying crops and villages and killing the inhabitants. Some of the survivors migrated westward.

The founding of the Ohio Company in 1787 to settle the Ohio Valley led to running fights with the remaining Shawnee and other Native Americans in the area. Defeat at the Battle of Fallen Timbers in 1794 meant that the Shawnee homelands on the Ohio were lost for good. The tribe split into three groups, the Absentee, Eastern, and Cherokee Shawnee. All eventually settled in Oklahoma.

SEE ALSO

FRENCH AND INDIAN WAR ■ IROQUOIS CONFEDERACY ■ PONTIAC ■ POPULATION, NATIVE-AMERICAN ■ RELIGION, NATIVE-AMERICAN

▼ *On July 9, 1755, a force of 900 French and native troops under Captain Daniel de Beaujeu attacked and defeated a 1,400-strong British force under General Braddock in the Ohio Valley. This action persuaded many Shawnee to ally with the French.*

SHAYS'S REBELLION

After the signing of the Treaty of Paris in 1783 the United States embarked on what seemed to many to be a critical period. During the 1780s the young nation appeared at times to be on the point of collapsing.

Independence meant an end to the lucrative trade within the British Empire, and the economies of some American states faced ruin. Many people feared a nationwide rebellion and did not believe the U.S. government could keep control in the event of such a revolt.

These fears nearly became a reality in January 1787, when a destitute farmer and Revolutionary War veteran from western Massachusetts named Daniel Shays led 1,200 debt-ridden farmers to Springfield, Massachusetts, to seize the federal armory. This desperate action to bring about change in the new republic by force of arms became known as Shays's Rebellion.

ECONOMIC DEPRESSION

During the 1780s Massachusetts was faced with having to repay large debts from the Revolutionary War and experienced a deep recession caused by the loss of trading links with Britain. In seven other American states where similar problems existed paper currency was issued to help debtors repay creditors. This helped alleviate many of the economic pressures felt by poor farmers and tradesmen, although their wealthy creditors received only paper currency that was likely to be devalued.

In Massachusetts, however, the state constitution rigidly restricted the vote to property holders, and this enabled wealthy Boston creditors to make laws that forced debtors to pay in hard currency. The legislature insisted on taxes being paid in hard currency as well. In western Massachusetts this resulted in many farmers being forced to pay up to one-third of their income in taxes, and those taxes could only be paid in hard currency. Unable to comply, hundreds of farmers were brought before courts, which often confiscated and auctioned their farms and livestock. Sometimes the farmers themselves were placed in debtors' prison.

When the Massachusetts legislature adjourned in 1786 without providing any tax relief or issuing any paper currency, farmers in Northampton, Massachusetts, erupted in revolt. The

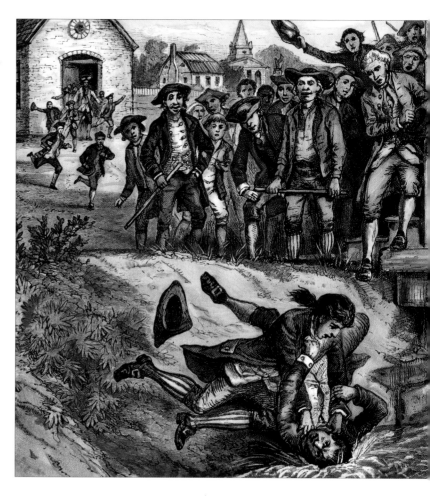

▲ *A group of townsfolk watch a fight between a supporter of the Massachusetts government and one of the rebels.*

rebellion spread quickly to four neighboring counties, and Daniel Shays emerged as the unlikely leader of the revolt. The rebels called themselves "Regulators" and wore sprigs of hemlock in their hats.

Governor James Bowdoin believed them to be a degenerate mob and asked the legislature to pass a riot act, which was issued on September 2. On September 26 Shays led 500 men to the courthouse at Springfield, where they forced an adjournment in proceedings. Across Massachusetts courthouses stopped meeting, effectively ending farm auctions and the loss of farmers' property.

Shays's followers narrowly escaped an encounter with the militia in November 1786, but in January of the next year Bowdoin, fearful of the mouting tensions, called out 4,000 state militia under General Benjamin Lincoln to protect the U.S. arsenal at Springfield. On January 25, 1,200 rebels attacked Springfield and tried to seize the arsenal. Both sides were very wary of firing on each other. When four rebels were killed by the militia, the remainder dispersed. The

rebels fled to Petersham in Vermont, where they were defeated by Lincoln's forces on February 4. Some of the captured leaders were subsequently sentenced to death, but none of the sentences was ever carried out. Daniel Shays was eventually pardoned on June 13, 1788.

GOVERNMENT REACTION

The rebellion had an immediate and profound effect on the ruling classes in America. George Washington was shocked that such an event could cloud the dawn of the republic.

Abigail Adams, wife of John Adams, criticized the rebels as a mob bent on tearing down the foundations of the republic. Stating her views in a letter to Thomas Jefferson, then in Paris as U.S. ambassador to France, she was shocked that Jefferson disagreed and infuriated by his radical response. Jefferson wrote that "the tree of liberty must be refreshed from time to time with the blood of patriots and tyrants."

When the Constitutional Convention met in Philadelphia in the summer of 1787, the violence and anarchy of the rebellion played an important role in convincing the delegates to increase the authority of the U.S. government in the Federal Constitution of 1787.

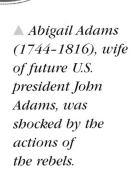

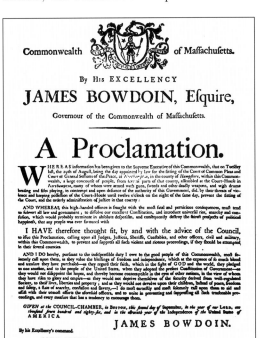

Abigail Adams (1744-1816), wife of future U.S. president John Adams, was shocked by the actions of the rebels.

A proclamation issued by the Massachusetts governor James Bowdoin on September 2, 1786, after the courthouse at Northampton had been briefly occupied by rebels. It warns Shays's followers of the illegality of their actions and urges law-abiding citizens to assist the militia.

SEE ALSO

ADAMS, JOHN ■ AMERICAN REVOLUTIONARY WAR ■ CONSTITUTIONAL CONVENTION

SLAVE CULTURE

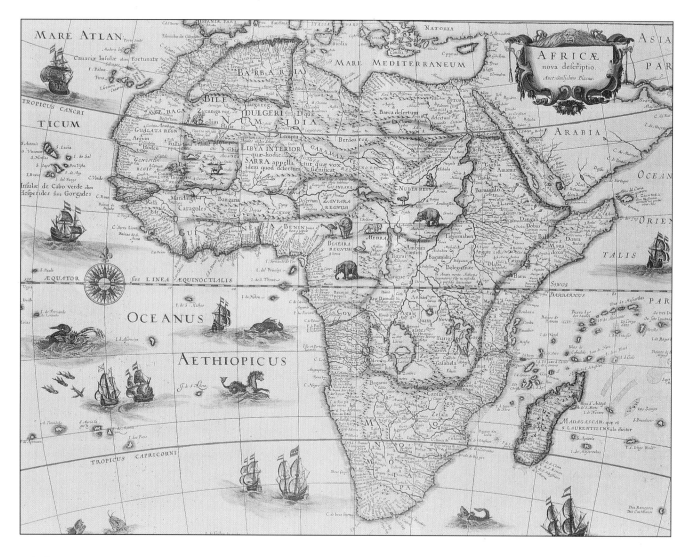

African-American culture varied widely across time and place, but by the time of the American Revolution a number of key features had emerged. The variety stemmed in part from the diverse religious and linguistic traditions of Africa and in part from the great differences between life in New England, New Netherland, the Chesapeake, South Carolina, and Spanish Florida.

African Americans, although barely two or three percent of the populations of colonial New Hampshire, Massachusetts, and Pennsylvania, made up more than half of all residents (at least at some times in the 18th century) in such places as eastern Virginia, South Carolina, and French (later Spanish) Louisiana. Most North Americans of African ancestry remained slaves at least until the end of the colonial era.

SPANISH COLONIES
The first Africans entered North America with Spanish explorers in the 16th century, long before the English settlements at Jamestown and Plymouth. Some came with Ponce de Leon's expedition to Florida in 1513. Estevanico was one African who

This 18th-century European map of Africa reveals a detailed knowledge of the African coastline, while the interior is poorly mapped.

accompanied Narvaez's expedition there in 1528. He later became the first African to explore parts of Arizona and New Mexico. Also in the early 1500s a group of African slaves ran away from a Spanish expedition and settled with a group of Native Americans in what is now Georgia or South Carolina. African people assisted European exploration in the Americas in many ways, and their experience in river navigation made them valuable as crewmen.

Two centuries later, in the 1720s and 1730s, an African slave named Francisco Menendez provided military leadership for Spanish Florida. He later successfully petitioned for freedom for himself and his fellow African soldiers, and led in the establishment of a black and Native-American village, Mose, just north of St. Augustine. During the years after the Revolutionary War an African American formerly from the French Caribbean, Jean Baptiste Du Sable, headed north from Louisiana to settle, trap, and trade at what later became known as Chicago, Illinois.

▼*This engraving shows an unusually spacious room in a Georgia slave dwelling.*

ENGLISH COLONIES

In the lands that eventually became the United States most of the history of African Americans, like most of the history of black slavery, took place in English-speaking America. The first African colonists appeared in the Chesapeake before 1620, and the first in New England before 1640. Their numbers remained scant, even in the southern colonies, until the late 17th century but grew rapidly in the first half of the 18th century.

When tens of thousands of Africans arrived in British North America, whether in Maryland and Virginia in the 1720s, or in Georgia and South Carolina as late as the 1790s, they brought with them vivid memories of the world they had left behind. They spoke various languages and came from varied societies. Gradually they forged a new culture, one that incorporated key features of their legacies from Africa as well as significant aspects of European and even Native-American cultures. Language and religion would long be the most apparent.

Slaves from Africa were not transported from Old World villages to New World plantations in their tribal or family groups. Because Africans spoke many different languages, slaves in Rhode Island, Virginia, and Georgia alike had to find a new means of communication. Most quickly learned enough English vocabulary to get by—to understand orders from masters and communicate with their fellows. The decline of the slave trade into the mainland British colonies (except Georgia and South Carolina) by the 1750s meant that there were few African immigrants encountering English for the first time. Yet in some areas, particularly along the rural coast of Georgia and South Carolina, African Americans were

S

either such recent arrivals, so numerous, or so routinely separate from whites that they continued to speak a dialect, now known as Gullah, for a long time. It is quite distinct from English.

Slowly during the colonial era African Americans in the British colonies began to embrace Protestant Christianity, just as their counterparts in French and Spanish America adopted Catholicism. The process was slow for various reasons. White settlers were reluctant to promote the gospel among slaves out of fear that conversion might render them in some ways whites' equals or might compromise their status as slaves. Slaves themselves often failed to see

the attractions of white religious beliefs, though the Great Awakening brought a more expressive form of religion that proved more attractive to whites and blacks alike. As late as the Revolutionary War only a small minority of African Americans had adopted Christianity, but the process continued to pick up strength until most blacks, slave or free, came to identify themselves as Baptists or Methodists, or some other variant of Protestant faith.

FAMILY LIFE

In kinship and family relationships African Americans created a culture that was not like that of their former homelands or of their white

▲ *This illustration shows slave quarters on a rice plantation. The little leisure time that slaves were allowed was devoted to family and friends.*

neighbors. Slaves had limited ability to protect themselves from decisions by their owners that could, without warning, split families forever. Parents might never again see their children or children their brothers and sisters. Partly for that reason, and partly to create relationships that might replace lost members of former communities, African Americans established broad kinship ties, whether based on blood and marriage or not, that could better promote a sense of community.

Whatever the specifics of family relationships, the end of the slave trade meant that most African Americans could create long-term relationships. The slave trade brought two or three men for each woman, but second-generation African Americans, born in the colonies, included as many women as men. By the time of the Revolutionary War slave communities were growing as fast as white communities through natural increase—more births than deaths. African-American families were as successful in raising large families of healthy children as were their white neighbors.

The slave family proved a central feature of African-American life. The law did not recognize slave marriages or inheritance, nor did it force owners to protect slave families from being broken up by the sale of one or more family members. The slaves themselves kept track of their own relationships. And the plantation owners found that supporting the institution of the slave family, up to a point, served their own purposes. Slave men with families were far less likely to take violent action against their owners, far less likely to seek escape from slavery alone, and far less likely to succeed if they tried to take their families.

▼ *These brick-built slave cabins stand on the grounds of Boone Hall Plantation in Mount Pleasant, South Carolina.*

S

African culture—from such economic activities as river navigation, cattle raising, and rice cultivation to such expressive activities as dance and music—made life in British North America something radically different from traditional life in Europe. For African Americans themselves the world they inhabited was made up of materials from the Old World and the New World alike.

The African-American culture of the 19th century had taken shape by the time white Americans gained their independence from Britain. By that time, too, larger numbers of African Americans—whether living in Massachusetts or Virginia—were beginning to gain their freedom from white ownership. More and more were beginning to live lives that, no longer so desperately shadowed by slavery, gave them space to shape their own ways.

SEE ALSO

LANGUAGE ■ PLANTATIONS ■ POPULATION, BLACK ■ SLAVE TRADE ■ SLAVERY ■ WEST INDIES

AFRICAN HERITAGE

People of African ancestry proved to be central to the history of colonial America. South Carolina's coastal plantations make the point as well as any New World phenomenon. At first many of the laborers in Carolina were European servants and Native-American slaves, but African-American slaves soon made up most of the labor force. They made possible the massive cultivation of rice and indigo—the major crops of 18th-century South Carolina—through far more than their labor alone. While the settlers knew nothing of growing rice, which was not much grown in Europe, the Africans knew a great deal about growing rice in Africa.

▲ *These slave chains, now in a European museum, are an enduring symbol of the cruel nature of slavery.*

▶ *Despite the soul-destroying conditions of their captivity, African slaves were able to maintain and develop their own distinctive culture.*

SLAVE TRADE

The tradition of slavery dates back to prehistoric times. Ancient civilizations from China and India to Greece and Rome depended on slave labor, especially in hazardous occupations such as construction and mining. Slaves in ancient times were usually prisoners of war and their families, who had been defeated in battle or conquered.

SLAVES AND SERFS

In Europe the institution of slavery died out after the collapse of the Roman Empire, and it was replaced by serfdom. Serfs were peasant farmers who were seen as belonging to the land they worked. They were required to work in their lord's fields for a certain number of days per year, pay him taxes on the fruits of their

▲ A European slave trader haggles over the purchase of slaves with an African slaver at the port of Goree in West Africa.

◀ Sickly and diseased slaves were likely to be thrown overboard in mid-Atlantic.

◀ *This painting shows the interior of a slave ship in the early 19th century. In earlier times slaves were often packed even more tightly together. The fresh air and light from the open hatch were a luxury that few slaves would experience.*

own labors, and even fight for him if required. Serfs could not be bought and sold, but their ownership could be transferred as part of a land transaction between lords.

EUROPE AND AFRICA

At the beginning of the 15th century Portuguese seafarers began questing along the western coast of Africa in search of gold and a possible sea route to Asia. As they sailed southward they encountered African chieftains who were happy to trade gold for the cloth and manufactured products carried by the Portuguese. If the chieftains had no gold metal in their treasuries, they offered slaves instead—"black gold."

Slavery was an everyday fact of life in Africa at that time. People were routinely captured and enslaved, and were bought and sold like any other commodity. Slave traders had existed in Africa long before the Europeans arrived, and initially Europeans had little impact on the African slave trade. Portuguese sailors took the first consignment of African slaves to Portugal in the mid-1400s, either as field laborers or household servants, but there was little demand for slaves in Europe.

▼ *This drawing shows the very close packing of the human cargo that was one of the typical features of the slave trade.*

AMERICAN TRADE

The discovery and subsequent exploitation of the New World produced a completely different situation. Spanish colonists in the Caribbean and Mexico, and the Portuguese in Brazil, quickly discovered that the Native Americans they encountered were poorly suited to forced labor and soon died. The slave traders of West Africa held the perfect solution—a seemingly endless supply of strong, healthy African slaves. The first African slaves were taken to the Caribbean in about the year 1500. During the next 300 years more than 10 million Africans would be transported in slavery across the

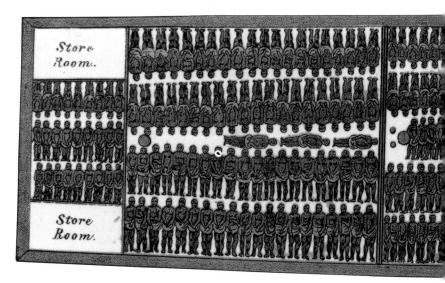

Store Room.

Store Room.

▶ *This map shows a simplified version of the triangular slave trade between the eastern seaboard of North America, Africa, and the islands of the Caribbean. Other ports, both in America and Africa, were also involved in the slave trade.*

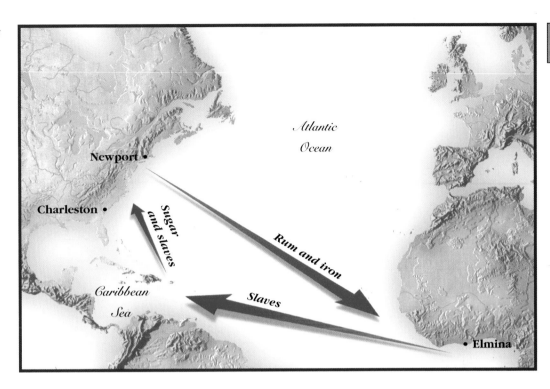

Atlantic to the New World. Most of them went to the Caribbean and South America; only about one in 20 ended up in the English-speaking colonies on the mainland.

The first African slaves to arrive in England's North American colonies were probably a group of 20 who were taken to Jamestown in 1619 on a Dutch ship. Historians are still not certain whether these people were actually slaves or were long-term indentured servants. Whatever the status of this Jamestown group, by the

late 17th century African slaves lived and worked in all the English colonies.

A TRIANGULAR TRADE

The slave trade developed rapidly during the second half of the 17th century and became part of the Triangular Trade—so-called because of the shape the trade routes make on a map of the Atlantic Ocean. Alcohol, iron, and other goods were taken from North America to West Africa, where they were traded with native chieftains for human cargoes. Slaves were loaded onto ships from great holding pens such as those at Elmina in present-day Ghana. From Africa the slaves were shipped across to the Caribbean islands, where the vast majority of them were sold. The third side of the Triangular Trade was the route from the Caribbean to the eastern seaboard colonies, which carried both slaves and sugar for the production of more alcohol.

The route across the Atlantic was known as the Middle Passage, and conditions on board ship were particularly horrifying. Ships' captains

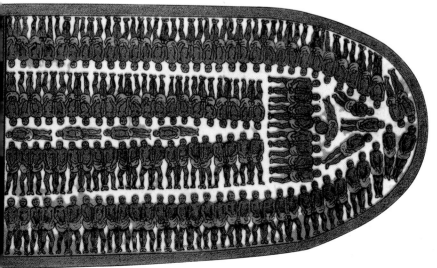

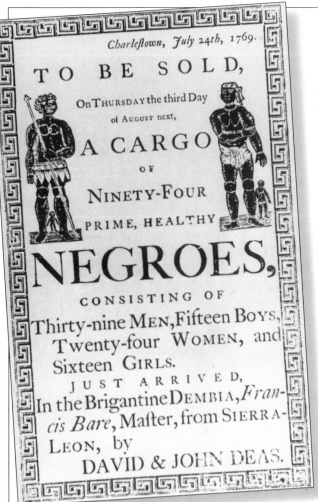

Charlestown, July 24th, 1769.

TO BE SOLD,

On THURSDAY the third Day
of AUGUST next,

A CARGO

OF

NINETY-FOUR

PRIME, HEALTHY

NEGROES,

CONSISTING OF

Thirty-nine MEN, Fifteen BOYS,
Twenty-four WOMEN, and
Sixteen GIRLS.

JUST ARRIVED,
In the Brigantine DEMBIA, Fran-
cis Bare, Master, from SIERRA-
LEON, by

DAVID & JOHN DEAS.

◄ This handbill advertises West African slaves who were to be sold by auction at Charleston, South Carolina, in July 1769.

became ill on voyage were thrown overboard. Once the ship had landed, the slaves were sold at auction.

CONTRACT SUPPLY

The Spanish empire in America did not import slaves directly. The Spanish authorities preferred to contract the supply of slaves to foreign trading companies, while insisting that the human cargo was carried on Spanish ships. The slave supply contract, which was an exclusive monopoly, was known as the *asiento*. In 1713, following the Treaty of Utrecht, the British South Sea Island company was awarded the monopoly for 30 years.

The ships, captains, and crews engaged in the slave trade had a variety of national origins, such as English, French, Dutch, Italian, and by the 18th century, American. Because the slave trade was extremely profitable, some slavers became rich and were able to build fine houses and establish family fortunes. After 1807 federal law outlawed the international slave trade into the United States.

often packed as many slaves as possible on their ships, knowing that a certain percentage would die during the voyage. There was often not enough room for the slaves to move around, and they usually spent the whole voyage lying down. There were no sanitary facilities, and disease was rife. They were fed the most meager of rations, with a little food twice a day. Traumatized by their captivity, slaves were sometimes reluctant to eat the food given to them. On one occasion a captain ordered his sailors to smash out the slaves' teeth and feed them by force. Sometimes the women were separated from the men, and they were often treated cruelly by the crews. The traders were, not surprisingly, more concerned about getting the slaves to the Americas quickly and selling them at a profit than anything else. Any who died or

▼ This spacious house was built in Medford, Massachusetts, in 1737 by the prominent British slave trader Isaac Royall.

SEE ALSO

NEW SPAIN ■ PLANTATIONS ■ POPULATION, BLACK ■ SLAVE CULTURE ■ SLAVERY ■ SUGAR ■ TOBACCO ■ WEST INDIES

SLAVERY

Slavery had existed in the Americas for over a century before the first Jamestown settlers arrived in 1607. As early as 1502 Spanish planters had purchased African slaves to work in the sugar fields of Hispaniola (modern Haiti). After 1513 the Spanish required that slave traders be licensed. They decided to purchase African slaves to perform agricultural and mining labor because diseases had decimated the native population.

PEOPLE AS PROPERTY

The conditions of slavery in the Americas were different from those of previous ages. Slavery in the New World was an economic institution. Slaveholders purchased slaves simply for their labor. Because of this most slaveholders only purchased male slaves to perform the arduous work on a plantation. Slaves were considered the property of their owners. Slaves were designated as chattels (moveable property) and lost their legal status as people.

Slaveholders could treat their slaves any way they wished. Generally slaves were treated very harshly. They worked from sunup to sundown and were often beaten for not working hard enough. Because slaves worked so much, were poorly housed, and poorly fed, many of them died. The mortality rate was particularly high on the Caribbean sugar plantations. As a result slaveholders needed to constantly replenish their labor force.

Initially planters acquired this unending supply of slaves from mainly Portuguese slave traders. The slave trade was centered on the West African coast. In the late 15th century, with their early voyages of exploration

along the West African coast, Europeans began participating in the enslavement of human beings. In the 16th century, with the increased demand for slaves in the New World, the slave trade took on new dimensions. Many more Africans were enslaved, and more families were forced apart.

Captives were sold to slave traders and then shipped across the Atlantic to the Spanish colonies in Central and South America. This cruel traffic in human beings was the primary source for labor during the first century of the colonization of America. About 95 percent of African slaves ended up in New Spain, but some were taken to the English colonies.

▲ *The arrival of a group of 20 Africans at Jamestown in 1619 is believed by many to mark the beginning of slavery in the English colonies. Some historians believe that the members of this group were not slaves but indentured servants.*

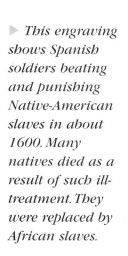

▲ *A group of chained and yoked slaves is escorted through the African bush by armed guards.*

SLAVES OR SERVANTS

When the English began colonizing Virginia, however, they initially opposed using slave labor. Instead of slavery they organized a system of indentured servitude. Under this system people had their passage to the English colonies paid for by planters. In exchange these indentured servants agreed to work for a specified term. In this manner the English poor and unemployed could find work and perhaps eventually become land owners.

Yet, like those of slaves, the lives of indentured servants were often harsh and short. Planters were uninterested in their servants' dreams of freedom and only wanted to get as much work out of them as possible. During their terms of service indentured servants were also treated as property. Unlike slaves, indentured servants never lost their legal status as people. Another difference between slaves and indentured servants was that if indentured servants survived their term of service, they became free.

▶ *This engraving shows Spanish soldiers beating and punishing Native-American slaves in about 1600. Many natives died as a result of such ill-treatment. They were replaced by African slaves.*

S

Slaves were held in bondage for life, and any children born to slaves were also considered slaves.

THE ENGLISH COLONIES

The English began importing slaves into their colonies during the first half of the 17th century. During the next few decades slavery existed alongside indentured servitude in the English colonies. Beginning in the island colonies of Barbados and Bermuda, however, colonial planters soon expressed a preference for slave labor. It is widely believed that these planters turned to slave labor because there was an insufficient number of people willing to emigrate from England as indentured servants.

In the island colonies the best land was rapidly claimed by the first settlers. This meant that many servants at the end of their terms had to migrate to the mainland colonies in order to find good farmland. Given the choice, most people who indentured themselves went to the Chesapeake colonies of Virginia and Maryland. By 1680, however, the Chesapeake colonies found themselves with a similar shortage of land. New colonies to the north attracted many immigrants who otherwise might have moved to the Chesapeake. Furthermore,

a decreasing death rate in the Chesapeake colonies made slave labor a better investment for the planters. Slavery was thus practiced by custom in the English colonies before it existed by law.

LAWS OF SLAVERY

Lacking any legal precedent from England, the individual colonies attempted to construct a legal stystem of slavery that defined slaves as the personal property of their owners. As early as 1636 in Barbados the governor's council had decreed that purchased Africans and Native Americans should work in a state of bondage for life unless a contract stipulated otherwise. However, this was simply a governor's decree and not a law. In 1641 in Massachusetts, and in 1650 in Connecticut, laws were passed that recognized slavery as

▼ *The Spanish missionary Bartolomé de las Casas had the official title Protector of Indians. He worked tirelessly to improve conditions for Native Americans and to prevent them from being enslaved.*

▲ *This painting shows a slave auction taking place in one of the English colonies.*

appropriate treatment for any non-Christian captives taken.

It was not until the latter half of the 17th century, however, that the colonies properly defined the legal nature of slavery. By 1670 Barbados, Virginia, Maryland, Jamaica, New York, and New Jersey had passed laws that not only recognized the legality of slavery but stated that the condition of slavery would be passed from mother to child.

By the early 18th century all of the British colonies had enacted legislation confirming the practice of slavery. Similar legislation was enacted in the French colonies at this time. The laws that confirmed the legality of slavery came at a time when the slave population was rapidly increasing in the British colonies. As the supply of indentured servants decreased, more planters purchased African slaves. The recent passage of laws reinforced and justified the absolute dominion of the master over his slaves. The power of life and death was central to the authority of the master. A 1669 Virginia law maintained that masters could not be charged with the murder of their slaves. This absolute authority made life for slaves miserable. Slaves could be beaten, maimed, violated, or even killed without any course of appeal. The master's will was law.

CONDITIONS OF SLAVERY

In the early 18th century most of the slaves imported into the British colonies had been transported from West Africa. After surviving the treacherous Middle Passage, slaves found themselves captives in a strange land. Only a very few African slaves could speak English. Probably even more distressing was the fact that many slaves could not initially communicate with each other. Although we speak of "African" slavery, it is important to remember that there was neither an "African" people nor language. African slaves came from many peoples and cultures, such as the Ibo, Yoruba, Dahomey, and Asante. Slaves were far from home and had no place to run away to safety. A few did, however, try to run away, and some were even successful, living off the land or taking refuge with sympathetic Native Americans. The majority of slaves remained in bondage, and only gradually were they able to construct an African-American culture.

Most slaves worked as agricultural laborers. Both men and women were made to work in the fields. The basic conditions of slaves' lives thus largely depended on what type of agricultural environment they were sold into. Generally, three distinct plantation systems operated in the British Colonies: sugar plantations in the West Indies, rice and indigo plantations in the South Carolina and Georgia lowcountry, and tobacco plantations in the Chesapeake region. The staple crop most often associated with slavery, cotton, was only grown in limited amounts during the colonial period and did not become popular until the 19th century.

Sugar plantations in the West Indies were large affairs that required a huge force of slave labor. It was not unusual for a sugar planter to own several hundred slaves. New slaves were always being purchased to replace those who had died.

Unlike the system of gang labor found in the West Indies, the rice and indigo plantations of Carolina were organized on a task system. Individual slaves were assigned series of tasks that had to be completed by a certain time. While the labor was still hard and the tasks numerous, slaves in Carolina often had time to tend their own gardens and produce their own foods. Disease from the lowlying swamps, however, had a serious effect on the life expectancy of the slaves and thus inhibited the development of slave communities.

Plantation owners in both the West Indies and Carolina were often absentee owners, staying away from their plantations for considerable lengths of time. As a result, slaves on these plantations rarely came in contact with their masters and usually dealt with an overseer instead.

Such was not the case in the Chesapeake tobacco plantations. In Maryland and Virginia slaveholders were resident owners. Most slaveholders owned fewer than five

EYEWITNESS

THIS EXTRACT FROM A PAMPHLET PUBLISHED IN 1746 PUTS FORWARD A VERY BRITISH VIEW OF SLAVERY IN THE AMERICAN COLONIES.

66 *Negroe Labor hitherto has supported our British Colonies, as it has done those of other Nations. It is Negroe Labor that also will keep them in due Subserviency to the Interest of their Mother Country; for while our Plantations depend only on Planting by Negroes, and that of such produce as interferes only with the Interests of our Rivals not of their Mother-Country, our Colonies can never prove injurious to British Manufacturers, never become independent of these Kingdoms, but remain a perpetual support to our European interest, by preserving to us a Superiority of Trade and Naval Power.* 99

slaves and oftentimes worked in the fields with their slaves. This close contact did not necessarily mean that these slaves experienced a milder form of bondage. In very real ways the masters' presence entered into every aspect of the slaves' lives.

▼ *A 17th-century planter and his family (with their finely dressed black servant) visit their slaves on the plantation.*

S

A
DIALOGUE,
CONCERNING THE
SLAVERY
OF THE
AFRICANS;
Shewing it to be the *Duty* and *Interest* of
the *American* Colonies to emancipate
all their *African* Slaves :

WITH AN

ADDRESS to the Owners of such Slaves.

DEDICATED TO THE HONORABLE THE
Continental Congress.

Open thy mouth, judge righteously, and plead the cause of
the poor and needy   PROV. XXXI. 9.
And as ye would that men should do to you, do ye also to
them likewise.   LUKE VI 31.

NORWICH:
Printed and sold by JUDAH P. SPOONER. 1776.

▲ *This pamphlet
was issued in
1776 to try to
persuade the
Continental
Congress to end
the practice of
slavery.*

▶ *The British
campaigner
Granville Sharp
was a vociferous
supporter of the
American colonies
and a tireless
advocate of
abolition.*

Even on the larger tobacco
plantations slaves rarely worked in
groups of more than ten. Planted
fields were often spread apart by
many miles on these plantations, and
the slave population was dispersed.
The lengthy process of preparing
tobacco meant that on the larger
plantations certain slaves developed
skills as coopers, blacksmiths, masons,
and carpenters.

The treatment of individual slaves,
however, depended entirely on the
whim of the owner. Some owners
abused their slaves, others did not.

ENDING SLAVERY

Public protests against slavery first
began appearing in the middle of the
18th century. The Society of Friends
(Quakers) was in the forefront of
abolitionism. The reform movement
soon spread throughout Britain and

into many of the colonies. Many
people in America were opposed to
slavery, especially in New England.
Even Virginia slaveowners such as
George Washington and Thomas
Jefferson expressed their dislike of
slavery in principle.

Following the Revolutionary War
many of the northern states passed
laws to abolish slavery. In 1808 both
Britain and the United States outlawed
the Atlantic slave trade. Ships of the
British navy patrolled the coast of
West Africa in an attempt to prevent
illegal slave trading.

In 1837 Britain abolished slavery in
the West Indies. Thus the southern
states stood alone as the last
slaveholding domain in the former
British colonies. Slavery finally ended
in the United States with the
Confederate defeat in the Civil War
(1861–1865) and the passage of the
Thirteenth Amendment, officially
proclaimed on December 18, 1865.

SEE ALSO
POPULATION, BLACK ■ RELIGION, QUAKER
■ SLAVE CULTURE ■ SLAVE TRADE ■ SUGAR
■ TOBACCO ■ WEST INDIES

CAPTAIN JOHN SMITH

John Smith was one of the founder members of the first permanent English settlement in North America at Jamestown in 1607. A skilled writer and mapmaker, he did more than any other man to encourage the first wave of English colonization.

Born in Lincolnshire, England, in 1580, Smith was a farmer's son who developed a taste for adventure while fighting in Europe as a young man. He was among the 100 or so Englishmen who landed at the site of Jamestown on May 14, 1607.

QUESTING SPIRIT

Despite his youth he soon became the leader of the group, organizing trade with the Native Americans and the building of houses, and making a number of river voyages that allowed him to produce the first accurate maps of Virginia. On one of these voyages he was captured by Native-American

▶ *John Smith became the elected president of the Jamestown colony council in September 1608, and under his direction the colony began to recover from its earlier setbacks.*

subjects of Powhatan and, according to legend, was saved from execution only by the intervention of Powhatan's 13-year-old daughter, Pocahontas.

In September 1609 Smith was injured when his gunpowder bag caught fire, and he was forced to return to England. When he had recovered, he contacted the Virginia Company of Plymouth with the aim of returning to North America. In 1614 he mapped the coastline of the area he named New England. The following year he made another voyage but was captured by pirates. After three months he escaped and returned to England penniless.

Smith made another attempt at colonization in 1617 that ended in complete failure; the ships, trapped by the wind, never left port. He never saw North America again but published maps and books about it until his death in 1631.

C. Smith taketh the King of Pamavnkee prifoner. 1608.

◀ *A picture from John Smith's* **Generall Historie of Virginia, New England and the Summer Isles,** *published in 1624, which shows Smith capturing the King of the Pamunkey tribe in 1608.*

SEE ALSO

JAMESTOWN ■ POCAHONTAS ■ POWHATAN ■ VIRGINIA COMPANY

SMUGGLING

Smuggling goods between the American colonies and their main export markets in Europe and the Caribbean escalated rapidly in the 18th century, as colonial merchants and planters sought to avoid the restrictive taxes imposed by the British parliament, which were cutting into their profits.

THE MOLASSES SMUGGLERS

In the summer of 1733 Parliament passed a tax law known as the Molasses Act. Molasses (a dark sugary liquid refined from sugar cane) was one of the main commodities necessary for the production of rum, a principal export from the North American colonies in the 18th century. The law stated that a sum of money was to be paid by colonial merchants on every gallon of molasses they imported that did not come from British-owned plantations. The act was designed to create a monopoly for British sugar planters in the West Indies. However, colonial merchants also relied heavily on sugar imports from Spanish and French colonies. If the law had been properly enforced, it would have sent sugar prices soaring, with a disastrous effect on the colonial rum industry and the young and fragile colonial economy.

However, the colonial customs system was badly organized. The British king and his ministers handed out the financially rewarding positions in the customs office to win political favor or to repay loyal politicians. A man's abilities as an administrator did not seem to matter much to them. These tax collectors were often inefficient and corrupt. Officials were so easy to bribe that smuggling from

the West Indies soon became widespread. A customs officer in Salem, Massachusetts, offered to let French molasses through for only 10 percent of the legal tax. Meanwhile, in New Jersey the tax collectors "entered into a composition [agreement] with Merchants and took only a Dollar a Hogshead [barrel] or some such small matter."

The fact that the Molasses Act failed to generate much revenue for the British proved to many of the king's advisers that the colonies were "lawless" and needed to be more strictly governed.

TOBACCO SMUGGLING

Export goods were also smuggled out of the colonies. Tobacco was the most important colonial export and was vital to the economies of Virginia and the Carolinas. The British parliament decreed that all exported tobacco had to pass through a British port, where it was taxed before it could be reexported to other countries. American merchants resented the added expense that this system,

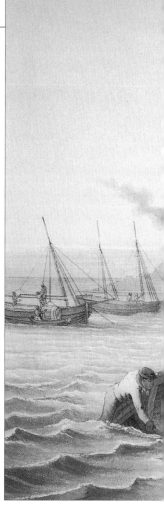

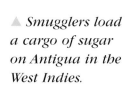
▲ *Smugglers load a cargo of sugar on Antigua in the West Indies.*

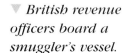
▼ *British revenue officers board a smuggler's vessel.*

encouraging the illegal traffic in smuggled goods. The customs system was extensively revised, and officials were given greater authority and protection from hostile merchants. However, the wily and resourceful smugglers continued to elude the attentions of the British.

Mostly the crews of American colonial ships appear to have obeyed British rules. This was especially true when they carried American goods from the colonies to Europe. From a purely practical standpoint they knew their own ships were easy to spot and could be overtaken and searched by the powerful British navy. Also, a large proportion of colonial sailors came from Massachusetts and Nantucket Island—strongholds of the Puritan religious faith. Their beliefs told them it was wrong to deny taxes to a king—even a resented British king. Furthermore, many of the merchants they dealt with were Quakers. Quakers were particularly insistent on the proper, legal conduct of business and did much to ensure that others kept within the law.

SEE ALSO
SUGAR ■ TAXES ■ TOBACCO ■ TRADE

known as enumeration, placed on their goods. They bypassed the system by landing their cargoes on deserted beaches far from the prying eyes of the customs men. Such was the extent of tobacco smuggling that in the 18th century more tobacco came into Britain illegally than legitimately. Spain was another popular market for tobacco smugglers. In 1744 there were approximately 40 vessels trading directly with the Spanish Empire.

THE SUGAR ACT

In 1764 the Sugar Act was passed by the British parliament, reducing the levy on foreign imports of molasses and other sugar products to the British colonies in North America. Parliament reasoned that by setting a lower rate of duty, it would be cheaper for colonial traders to import their goods legally than to smuggle them. The act also imposed duties on foreign cloth, indigo, coffee, and wine, further

▼ *Smugglers used caves along the coast of Britain to hide their cargoes.*

SOCIAL STRUCTURE

Although the British colonies in North America were more egalitarian than most places in the world on the eve of the Revolutionary War, their people did not enjoy true social equality. There were definite classes of people, and for the most part, it was the men with the land and the money who ruled the colonies. However, the realities of life in the New World had started to break down the rigid class structure that had been inherited from European society.

NEW SOCIAL STRUCTURE

Very few of England's ruling aristocratic families emigrated to the hostile wilderness of North America. With a few exceptions, such as the Fairfax family of Virginia, most of the English colonies' upper class came from the landed gentry—a class of wealthy landowners in England. Some were younger sons of aristocrats in England, where the oldest son traditionally inherited all his father's property. Others came from wealthy families that had no aristocratic titles. Families like the Winthrops, the Saltonstalls, and the Dunlaps in Massachusetts, the Randolphs and the Washingtons in Virginia, and the Carrolls in Maryland formed colonial America's politically powerful and influential elite.

SOCIAL CLIMBERS

Although the wealthiest families tended to cling to their position on the social ladder, the structure of colonial American society was less rigid than in Europe. There were far more opportunities in the New World for individuals to move up in life. This was particularly true in Virginia, where

a man like William Byrd, the son of an English goldsmith, could become rich through the tobacco, fur, and rum trades. He acquired more than 23,000 acres (9,308 ha) of land and became one of the most influential men in the colony. His son, William Byrd II, expanded his father's holdings to 180,000 acres (72,720 ha).

John Carter came to Virginia from an even lower social standing in 1649, but by the end of the 18th century his descendants were among the wealthiest in America. One of the family, dubbed "King Carter," owned 300,000 acres (121,200 ha) of land, 1,000 slaves, an ironworks, a mill, and a library of 1,500 books.

In the colony of New York Kiliaen Van Rensselaer, the son of an Amsterdam jewel merchant, and Robert Livingston, the son of a poor Scottish minister, did so well that the two families together owned more than one million acres (404,000 ha) in the 18th century.

WEALTH AND INFLUENCE

Money and land were the route to a higher social standing. A man who

▲ *The Byrd family mansion in Westover, Virginia.*

▼ *Artisans enjoying themselves in a colonial tavern.*

had both could expect political favors and appointments in the colonial government. Lucrative government contracts to supply the British with, for example, naval stores would also be exchanged between those at the upper end of the social scale. This served to cement their financial and political dominance.

Merchants who succeeded at turning a profit could also expect to rise to the top of society, with all the benefits that entailed. Merchant dynasties developed in port cities like Boston, New York, Philadelphia, and Charleston. John Hull of Boston was so successful that he opened up his own mint and made coins.

Although they were rarely as wealthy as merchants and landowners, men in the legal, medical, and ecclesiastical professions often socialized with the colonial aristocracy and were considered in, or nearly in, the same social class. Church ministers were always on this level, and by the mid-18th century lawyers and doctors had also taken their place in the

upper classes. John Adams and Thomas Jefferson, whose fathers had been middle-class farmers, were both lawyers. Both were accepted into the upper levels of colonial society.

The only place in the colonies where the social structure was in any way more equal, regardless of money or social background, was in New England. Here the land was divided among modest farms. Almost all white men were allowed to vote. But equality did not please everyone. One colonist complained that in Massachusetts the wealthy landowners could not rule as they believed they had the right to because the poorer landowners outvoted them. In most other colonies there was a requirement for a man to own a certain amount of land to be able to vote or to stand for election. In practice this meant few men were able to participate in government.

YEOMEN, ARTISANS, AND SLAVES
Farmers who owned less substantial tracts of land than the gentry were known as yeomen. They worked in the fields rather than relying entirely on hired or slave labor. Yeomen were proud of their place in society and addressed each other as "Goodman"

▲ Carried in a sedan chair, a wealthy lady is introduced to a neighbor's child. Plantation society in the southern states had all of the refinement and polite mannerisms of European society.

S

and "Goodwife." They formed a distinct social group with the artisans. Artisans were master craftsmen, such as silversmiths, barrel makers, glass blowers, and potters with established, profitable businesses in towns.

Below them were the landless farmers who hired themselves out to work for others and journeymen, craftsmen who had not yet settled down in their own shops. Below the landless farmers were the indentured servants, who were held on temporary contracts as workers on the farms or in the households of others. At the very bottom of the social ladder were the many thousands of African-American and Native-American slaves who were held in enforced captivity for their entire lives and the lives of their descendants.

NEW SPAIN AND NEW FRANCE

In New Spain intermarriage between Europeans, Native Americans, and African Americans had always been accepted. Racial prejudice was less pronounced, but a clear social order based on skin color (a pigmentocracy) developed with the white Spanish elite at the top.

New France was settled under a system in which landholders, called *seigneurs*, worked their land through the labor of tenants, called *habitants*. Tenants were tied to the land and owed their welfare and allegiance to the seigneurs. Seigneurs were given respect and deference, but the actual social gap between the two groups was smaller than it might seem. Although New France had no assemblies or elections, the seigneurial system created a rather classless society.

UNEQUAL SOCIETY

Colonial Americans, particularly in the English colonies, were very aware of social class. The men at the top of the ladder often put the word "Esquire" after their name, while those just under them earned the right to put "Mister" in front of their name. These people lived a priviledged and pampered life style.

From the top to the bottom of society the American colonies were very unequal. New England was a little more equality-minded, but this was only true for white men. Women, Native Americans, and African Americans were much less equal than their white male counterparts. Nonetheless the New World was, as one person described it, "the best poor man's country in the world."

▲ *Miss Evelyn Byrd was a member of one of the wealthiest and most powerful families in colonial America.*

◀ *Richard Lee was a merchant who first arrived in York County, Virginia, in 1641. He built up a substantial estate and fortune from his business.*

SEE ALSO

GOVERNMENT, COLONIAL ▦ IMMIGRATION, ENGLISH ▦ LAND ▦ MERCHANTS ▦ NEW FRANCE ▦ NEW SPAIN

SONS OF LIBERTY

In the summer of 1765 a law was passed in the British parliament that put a tax on all printed matter in the American colonies. This included newspapers, pamphlets, legal documents, licenses— even playing cards. The law was known as the Stamp Act. To many colonists it seemed an unfair way for the British parliament to raise money for its own use. It was also the first time Britain had taxed the colonies directly— and looked like a bad omen for the future.

RADICAL TACTICS

Radical colonial leaders were outraged. Paul Revere and Samuel Adams in Massachusetts, together with John Lamb and Alexander McDougall in New York,

were already talking of Britain's arrogant attitude toward the colonies. The Stamp Act seemed to bear out their words. They therefore set about forming secret organizations to resist the tax. The members of these groups called themselves the Sons of Liberty, taking their name from a phrase used in a speech made against the Stamp Act in Parliament.

The measures adopted by the Sons of Liberty—or "Liberty Boys," as they became known—were simple. They first sought to scare stamp agents, or tax collectors, and people who were

prepared to pay the tax. For example, they issued placards to demonstrators that read, "The First Man that either distributes or makes use of Stampt Paper, let him take care of his House, Person, and Effects." ("Stampt Paper" referred to paper that had been specially marked to show that the tax had been paid.)

When the scare tactics did not work, the Liberty Boys resorted to violence. In New York, for instance, Major Thomas James, the British officer who had charge of the official stamps, promised that "the stamps

▲ *At Golden Hill, New York, in late 1769 the Sons of Liberty battled with British soldiers who had chopped down a Liberty Pole they had erected. The New Yorkers were angered that soldiers were taking jobs and marrying local women.*

The true Sons of Liberty

And Supporters of the Non-Importation

Agreement,

ARE determined to refent any the leaft Infult or Menace offer'd to any one or more of the feveral Committees appointed by the Body at Faneuil-Hall, and chaftife any one or more·of them as they deferve ; and will alfo fupport the Printers in any Thing the Committees fhall defire them to print.

☞AS a Warning to any one that fhall affront as aforefaid, upon fure Information given, one of thefe Advertifements will be pofted up at the Door or Dwelling-Houfe of the Offender.

Liberty Boys usually met by night at so-called Liberty Poles, or Liberty Trees, which became the symbols of their struggle. They continued to attack Crown officials until the outbreak of the Revolutionary War, even fighting with redcoats on the streets of New York in 1769. Their resistance to the Stamp Act and their willingness to use violence against the colonial administration were a critical step in the direction of American independence.

SEE ALSO
ADAMS, JOHN ■ ADAMS, SAMUEL ■ AMERICAN REVOLUTIONARY WAR ■ REVERE, PAUL ■ STAMP ACT CRISIS

◀ *The Sons of Liberty deliver a stern warning to anyone who opposes them.*

▼ *A pamphlet printed in Boston in 1765 calling on colonists to boycott a local trader.*

would be crammed down New Yorkers' throats." The Liberty Boys responded by stirring up a mob, which broke into the major's house, drank all his wine, and smashed his furniture and china.

In Boston there was even more trouble than in New York. The Liberty Boys burned the records of the vice-admiralty court, ransacked the house of the Controller of Currency, and burned and looted the mansion of Governor Thomas Hutchinson.

ANGER BOILS OVER

These crude methods were highly successful. Almost all the stamp agents in the colonies gave up their jobs even before the act came into effect in November 1765. However, not everyone on the colonial side agreed with the advocates of violence. The lawyer John Adams, himself a harsh critic of the act, remarked sadly that "when the pot is set to boil, the scum rises to the top."

WILLIAM JACKSON,

an *IMPORTER*; at the

BRAZEN HEAD,

North Side of the TOWN-HOUSE,

and *Oppofite* the *Town-Pump, in*

Corn-hill, BOSTON.

It is defired that the SONS and DAUGHTERS of *LIBERTY,* would not buy any one thing of him, for in fo doing they will bring Difgrace upon *themfelves*, and their *Pofterity*, for *ever* and *ever,* AMEN.

SOUTH CAROLINA

The first Europeans to land on the South Carolina coast were a group of about 600 Spanish settlers who established the colony of San Miguel de Guadalupe in October 1526. The colony was abandoned after only a few months. Fort Santa Elena on Parris Island was established by the Spanish in 1566, but this, too, was soon abandoned. On March 24, 1663, the English king, Charles II, granted title to America south to 29° and north to 36°30' to eight English proprietors.

In March 1669 the proprietors issued a document, known as the

CAROLINA'S CONSTITUTION

Under the terms of the Fundamental Constitutions the Carolina colony was to be divided into counties of 480,000 acres (193,920 ha). Within a county each of the eight proprietors would hold 12,000 acres (4,848 ha), two West Indian planters would each have 24,000 acres (9,696 ha.), and four other planters would each have 12,000 acres (4,848 ha). The remaining 60 percent of the land was to be divided into freeholdings of varying sizes.

The proprietors and planters were to hold their own courts with themselves as judges, and the oldest resident proprietor was to be governor. There was to be an elected assembly, but only people owning more than 500 acres (202 ha) could stand for election. The documents were partly written by the English philosopher John Locke, but they were never approved by the colonial assembly and were formally withdrawn in 1691.

▲ *This cannon at Fort Moultrie in Charleston was used to repulse the British invasion fleet on June 28, 1776.*

Fundamental Constitutions of Carolina, outlining their plans for the colony's social and political structure.

After several failed attempts at starting a colony, the proprietors funded a party of 148 settlers from England and the Caribbean island of Barbados. They founded Charles Town (later known as Charleston) in April 1670 at Albemarle Point on the west bank of the Ashley River. Ten years later the town moved to a harbor site at Oyster Point, between the Ashley and Cooper rivers.

Most of the founders of Charles Town were of English origin. English immigrants and their American-born descendants formed the largest part of the population throughout the colony's history. In 1671 Dutch colonists from New York moved to the South Carolina coast. French

S

The colony's policy of religious toleration also brought a small Jewish enclave to Charleston. A thriving slave trade (40 percent of all the Africans brought to the British colonies in North America passed through Charleston) meant that during the 18th century there was a black majority in the colony. A large number of German immigrants settled in the backcountry, and after the defeat of the Highland clans by the British in 1746 a wave of Scots arrived.

The settlement of Clarendon County, as the southern part of Carolina was known, was at first confined to the coastal plain. Farming allowed the people to become self-sufficient, but rather than grow cash crops, they preferred to trade in animal skins with the local Native Americans. The Barbadians also took to enslaving the natives.

SOUTH CAROLINA'S ECONOMY

The early economy was largely based on exports of beef. Rice was introduced in the 1690s by sugar plantation owners from Barbados. It grew particularly well in the coastal tidewater region and became the chief

Arthur Middleton (1742-1787) was at the forefront of the independence movement in South Carolina.

Protestants, known as Huguenots, came in the 1680s to escape religious persecution in their homeland and created many successful businesses.

The Drayton Hall Plantation was built between 1738 and 1742 on the Ashley River in Charleston. It was designed in the Georgian style popularized by wealthy English landowners.

source of revenue during the 18th century. Indigo had become an important export by the mid-18th century, while the woodlands provided valuable naval stores.

CROWN CONTROL

During Queen Anne's War (1702–1713) there were border skirmishes with the Spanish in Florida, and in 1715 the Creek and Yamasee tribes attacked and killed more than 400 settlers and at one point threatened Charleston itself.

In 1719 years of dispute between the colonists and the proprietors erupted into a popular revolt. This partly resulted from the failure of the owners to organize effective defenses against Spanish and native attacks. Two years later South Carolina came under Crown control after the colonists had overthrown the proprietors' government. In 1729 South Carolina was formally granted a royal charter. After 1730 the interior began to be settled, but instead of creating new parishes, the colony's legislature simply extended existing coastal parish boundaries. This meant that backcountry residents had to

travel long distances to get a marriage license or register land claims. There was virtually no law and order; the deputies were often in league with criminals, and there were no courts.

In this atmosphere of lawlessness law-abiding citizens refused to pay taxes until they gained representation in the assembly. In the meantime they set up vigilante societies called Regulators to track down lawbreakers, who were often executed on the spot.

Though courts were instituted in the back country in 1769, the dispute was still simmering at the outbreak of the Revolutionary War in 1775. On June 28, 1776, a British fleet attacked Charleston but was severely damaged by gunfire from Fort Moultrie and withdrew. However, in May 1780 a

▲ *The John Stuart house, built in 1772, is one of the best-preserved merchants' houses in Charleston.*

S

◀ *Old Mill Gap Road is on the site of the Battle of Cowpens in South Carolina. On January 17, 1781, General Daniel Morgan's army of Patriots routed the British forces here.*

British force under General Clinton captured Charleston and occupied the town until October 1782. In 1779 British troops tried without success to invade the colony through Georgia, and throughout the remainder of the war the Continental Army under Nathaneal Greene fought a war of attrition against British forces in South Carolina. On May 23, 1788, South Carolina became the eighth state to ratify the Constitution.

A NEW ARISTOCRACY

The export of rice and indigo and the trade in slaves made some South Carolinians rich in the 18th century. Landed families lived the lives of the English nobility, hunting, fishing, and hosting lavish parties in their plantations along the tidewater rivers. Charleston, the trading center of the whole southern coast, became a social center to match older towns such as Philadelphia and Boston. In fall and winter members of this new aristocracy—families such as the Pinckneys, Draytons, Rutledges, and Manigaults—went there for the sitting of the assembly and spent their free time socializing and keeping up with the latest London fashions in clothes and furniture.

STAMP ACT CRISIS

During the 1700s the colonies in America were a highly important part of the British economy. Trade with the colonies was extensive and extremely profitable. Goods such as tobacco were in huge demand throughout Europe, and their distribution brought large revenues to the British Exchequer. The North American colonies were also an extremely valuable market for British export goods.

Nevertheless, protracted warfare in the 1750s between Britain and France, and the significant expenses involved in defending the American colonies, persuaded the British government to take full advantage of its powers and raise additional revenue through taxation in the American colonies.

A NEW TAX

In 1765 the British prime minister George Grenville suggested that a new form of taxation could be applied and justified on the grounds that the money would be used to establish and maintain military defenses for the colonies. His idea was that all legal documents, licenses, commercial contracts, newspapers, pamphlets, and even playing cards (card playing and gambling on cards were popular pastimes in the colonies) would have to carry a tax stamp. In order for people to make documents legal, or to buy such a simple thing as a newspaper, they would have to pay a tax for the privilege of doing so.

Far from being luxuries, many of these things were absolutely necessary for people to carry on doing business and run their everyday lives. This increased the attractiveness of the tax to the British politicians because it

promised a high return for relatively little cost in terms of administration and collection. In this apparently simple way the British government would be able to collect money from the colonies to add to their coffers.

The members of the British parliament found little to criticize in the plan, and the majority of them voted the tax into law. People in Britain were also affected by the tax, which had been operating in Britain for some time when it was applied to the American colonies in March 1765.

When news of the decision reached America, the colonists were infuriated.

▲ *The first page of the Stamp Act of 1765, bearing the name and title (in Latin) of the British king, George III. The tax, for all the trouble it caused, raised only a tiny amount of revenue.*

S They felt that it was simply unjust that the British should be allowed to impose such a tax on people who had no representatives in Parliament to argue on their behalf. Their opposition went even further: if their views were not represented in Parliament, they claimed, then the British government could not legally tax them at all.

CIVIL UNREST

The Stamp Act caused a storm in America. People were outraged at what they considered to be the arrogance of the British government. A secret group called the Sons of Liberty formed the opinion that only direct physical opposition would be appropriate. They began a campaign of physical violence against those involved in imposing the new law on the people of the colonies. Many of the men whose job it was to enforce the law were physically

attacked by mobs of protesters and had their property destroyed. This opposition was not confined to one or two of the colonies but spread across most of the New England and middle colonies. Many colonial assemblies passed resolutions against the Stamp Act.

▲ *Colonists burn official documents marked with the hated stamp.*

STAMP ACT CONGRESS

The leaders of the colony of Massachusetts had the idea of uniting the colonies in a single body to make an official protest, so they invited representatives from all the British colonies to join them at a congress to be held in New York City. Their hope was that, while the British might be able to dismiss the violence and disorder of the Sons of Liberty as the work of an unrepresentative rabble, they would be compelled to listen to

◀ *Stamps such as these became symbols of British oppression. The upper embossed mark records a tax in shillings, while the lower one represents a halfpenny tax.*

the protests of official representatives of the colonies. On October 7 men from Massachusetts, New York, New Jersey, Rhode Island, Pennsylvania, Delaware, Connecticut, Maryland, and South Carolina convened to discuss the developing crisis. During two weeks of discussions they drew up a series of documents to explain and underline to the British government their hostility to the new tax and their reasons for opposing it.

The most important of these documents was the *Declaration of Rights and Grievances*, but an address to the king and a group of petitions to the British parliament were also drafted. However, Parliament refused to recognize the congress as a legitimate body and would not consider any of its petitions.

Despite this setback, the colonists' rallied to the slogan "No taxation without representation," and opposition to the Stamp Act grew.

On October 31, 1765, a group of New York merchants signed the Nonimportation Agreement, in which they agreed not to import British goods. This had a huge impact on transatlantic trade and on the profits of British merchants and traders. These wealthy and politically influential men lobbied the British parliament until the Stamp Act was repealed in March the next year.

The episode is important in that it revealed significant limits to the power of the British government in North America and showed the collective power the colonies might wield if they stood together.

SEE ALSO

MERCHANTS ▪ SONS OF LIBERTY ▪ TAXES ▪ TRADE

▼ *This American cartoon mocks the repeal of the Stamp Act on March 18, 1766. The cartoonist ridicules the British customs officials and judges as they return to Britain.*

FURTHER READING

Anderson, Joan. **A Williamsburg Household**. *New York: Clarion Books, 1988.*

Barrett, Tracy. **Growing up in Colonial America**. *Brookfield, Connecticut: The Milbrook Press, 1995.*

Bosco, Peter L. **Roanoke: The Lost Colony**. *Brookfield, Connecticut: The Milbrook Press, 1992.*

Bowen, Gary. **Stranded at Plimoth Plantation 1629**. *New York: HarperCollins Publishers, 1994.*

Carter, Alden R. **The Colonial Wars**. *New York: Franklin Watts, 1992.*

Clare, John D., ed. **The Voyages of Christopher Columbus**. *San Diego: Gulliver Books (HBJ), 1992.*

Daugherty, James. **The Landing of the Pilgrims**. *New York: Random House, 1978.*

Erdosh, George. **Food & Recipes of the 13 Colonies**. *New York: PowerKids Press, 1997.*

Fritz, Jean. **The Double Life of Pocahontas**. *New York: Puffin Books, 1983.*

Hakim, Joy. **The First Americans**. *New York: Oxford University Press, 1993.*

Hakim, Joy. **Making Thirteen Colonies**. *New York: Oxford University Press, 1993.*

Hakim, Joy. **From Colonies to Country**. *New York: Oxford University Press, 1993.*

Kalman, Bobbie. **Colonial Life**. *New York: Crabtree Publishing, 1992.*

Kalman, Bobbie. **Historic Communities: A Colonial Town—Williamsburg**. *New York: Crabtree Publishing, 1992.*

Kent, Deborah. **African Americans in the Thirteen Colonies**. *New York: Childrens Press, 1988.*

Lenski, Lois. **Indian Captive: The Story of Mary Jemison**. *New York: HarperTrophy, 1969.*

Roach, Marilynne K. **In the Days of the Salem Witchcraft Trials**. *Boston: Houghton Mifflin Co., 1996.*

Roop, Connie and Peter, eds. **Pilgrim Voices: Our First Year in the New World**. *New York: Walkers and Company, 1995.*

Tunis, Edwin. **Shaw's Fortune: The Picture Story of a Colonial Plantation**. *Cleveland: The World Publishing Company, 1966.*

Speare, Elizabeth George. **The Witch of Blackbird Pond**. *Boston: Houghton Mifflin Co., 1958.*

Washburne, Carolyn Kott. **A Multicultural Portrait of Colonial Life**. *New York: Marshall Cavendish, 1994.*

Waters, Kate. **Tapenum's Day: A Wampanoag Indian Boy in Pilgrim Times**. *New York: Scholastic Press, 1996.*

Yenne, Bill, ed. **Our Colonial Period: The Chronicle of American History from 1607 to 1770**. *San Francisco: Bluewood Books, 1996.*

SET INDEX

Volume numbers and main entries are shown in **bold**. Page numbers of illustrations or captions are shown in *italic* or ***bold italic*** if they are in main articles.

**The editors wish to thank Peter Wallenstein, Associate
Professor of History at Virginia Polytechnic Institute and
State University, for his help in preparing this volume.**

Picture Credits
AKG London/Archivo General de Indias, Seville 656 **The
Bridgeman Art Library**/British Library 682t Library Company of
Philadelphia 674t **Corbis**/William A.Bake 705 Bettmann front
cover, title page, 649b, 654t, 657t, 665, 667, 668, 680, 683, 688-9b,
691, 694, 697t, 701t, 703 Library of Congress cover, 654b, 658t,
659t, 672b, 673, 674b, 677, 679, 682b, 687b, 692b, 693, 700-1b,
706t Lowell Georgia 649t Angelo Hornak 676 Dave G.Houser 669t
Liz Hymans 662b Wolfgang Kaehler 707 Kelly/Mooney
Photography 645b David Muench 661, 708 Gianni Dagli Orti 687t
Lee Snider 646, 685, 690b, 700t J.Sohm/ChromoSohm Inc. 706b

Adam Woolfitt 686t **ET Archive** 699t National Maritime Museum
688t **Mary Evans Picture Library** 645t, 647, 675, 684, 686b, 696b,
710 **Angelo Hornak Library** 658b **Hulton Getty** 652, 655b, 670t,
681t, 692t **The Natural History Museum, London** 671 **Peter
Newark's American Pictures** 644, 648, 650, 651, 653, 655t, 657b,
662t, 663, 664, 666, 669b, 670b, 672t, 681b, 690t, 695, 696t, 697b,
698, 699b, 702, 704, 709, 711

Map by John Woolford: 689
Artwork by John Egan: 678